Milena

Milena

The Tragic Story of Kafka's Great Love

Margarete Buber-Neumann

Translated from the German by
Ralph Manheim

Arcade Publishing • New York

FIRST ARCADE PAPERBACK EDITION

Library of Congress Cataloging-in-Publication Data
Buber-Neumann, Margarete, 1901–1989
    [Kafkas Freundin Milena. English]
    Milena : the tragic story of Kafka's great love / Margarete Buber-
Neuman; translated from the German by Ralph Manheim. —1st
Arcade   PB ed.
        p.   cm.
    ISBN 1-55970-390-3
    1. Kafka, Franz, 1883–1924—Relations with women. 2. Milena,
1896–1944. 3. Authors, Austrian—20th century—Biography. 4.
Journalists—Czech Republic—Biography. 5. Buber-Neumann,
Margarete, 1901– 6. Ravensbrück (Concentration camp) 7. World
War, 1939–1945—Prisoners and prisons, German. 8. Political pris-
oners—Germany—Biography. I. Title
PT2621.A26Z64613   1997
833'.912—dc21   97-26760

Published in the United States by Arcade Publishing, Inc., New York,
by arrangement with Seaver Books
Distributed by Little, Brown and Company

10 9 8 7 6 5 4 3 2 1

BP

PRINTED IN THE U.S.A.

CONTENTS

ACKNOWLEDGMENTS

I wish to thank all of Milena's friends who helped me with this book, above all Wilma Lövenbach for her untiring advice and assistance; Arthur Koestler, Paul Rütti, Willy Haas, Joachim von Zedtwitz, Jaroslav Dressler, Miloš Vaněk, Anička Kvapilová, and all those who shared their memories with me or provided me with background material.

Many sources of information about Milena's life have been closed to me as a German without knowledge of the Czech language. I am unfamiliar with Czechoslovakia and the city of Prague. I have my conversations with Milena to thank for whatever I know about the marvelous cultural flowering in her Czech homeland during her lifetime, the first thirty years of this century. I met Milena in a concentration camp. It was there that she told me of her past life. For that reason, my account may not be free from inaccuracies, for which I apologize. It was only after long hesitation that I undertook the perilous venture of writing this book. I did so because I was fascinated by Milena's personality and because of the profound friendship that united us.

*She is living fire, such as I had never seen. . . . At the same time
extremely affectionate, courageous and intelligent. She puts all that
into her sacrifice or, if you prefer, comes by it through sacrifice. . . .*

—FRANZ KAFKA

1

MEETING AT
THE WAILING WALL

I received Milena's first letter on October 21, 1940; someone
slipped it into my hand while I was walking on the camp street.
We had known each other for only a few days. But what can
days mean when time is counted not in hours and minutes, but
in heartbeats?

We met in the women's concentration camp at Ravensbrück.
Milena had heard about me from a German woman who had
arrived at the camp in the same shipment as herself. The journalist Milena Jesenská wanted to talk to me; she wished to know
if it was true that the Soviet Union had really handed over
antifascist refugees to Hitler. Milena approached me during the
newcomers' exercise period on the narrow path between the
backs of the barracks and the high wall topped with electrified
barbed wire. "Milena from Prague," she said by way of introduction. Her native city meant more to her than her surname.
I shall never forget the strength and grace of the gesture with
which she gave me her hand. When her hand was in mine, she
said with a tinge of irony, "Please don't give me one of your
German handshakes. My fingers are sore." Her face was prison-
gray, marked with suffering. But my impression of illness was
dissipated by the light in her eyes and the force of her movements. Milena was a tall woman with broad, straight shoulders
and fine features. Her eyes and chin revealed energy and her

beautifully curved lips a superabundance of emotion. Her delicately feminine nose suggested fragility, and the earnestness of her rather prominent forehead was attenuated by its frame of small curls.

The path was narrow and we were in the way, obstructing the other prisoners in their movements to and fro. Muttering angrily, they kept trying to push us forward. I wanted nothing more than to get our greetings over with as quickly as possible and fall back into the prescribed "exercise" rhythm. In years of imprisonment I had adapted to these herd movements. Of this, Milena was utterly incapable. Here in the concentration camp she behaved exactly as if we had been introduced on a boulevard in some peaceful city. Carried away by the pleasure of making a new acquaintance or perhaps by the curiosity of the born reporter, she ignored the grumbling all around us and prolonged our amenities as much as possible. At first her insouciance infuriated me. But soon I was fascinated and delighted. Here was an unbroken spirit, a free woman in the midst of the insulted and injured.

After that we walked along with the others, back and forth at the foot of the "Wailing Wall" (as Milena called it), while the dust raised by our wooden clogs swirled all around us. When you meet someone under normal conditions, the way he is dressed usually tells you something about him. "Milena from Prague" was wearing the same long, striped, bulky dress as I, the same blue apron and regulation headscarf. I knew nothing about her except that she was a Czech journalist. She spoke with a slight Czech accent, but her German was otherwise perfect; even in the first few minutes of our acquaintance I was enormously impressed by her vocabulary and gift of expression.

After a few parting words and the usual *Auf Wiedersehen* I went back to my barracks. All the rest of the day I was blind and deaf to everything. I was full of the name "Milena," drunk on the sound of it.

My feelings can only be appreciated by one who has been lonely in the midst of a great crowd. I had been shipped to Ravensbrück early in August 1940. Behind me I had years of terror in the Soviet Union. Arrested in Moscow by the NKVD and sentenced to five years at forced labor, I was taken to Karaganda, a concentration camp in Kazakhstan. Then in 1940 the Russian state police handed me over to the Gestapo, who questioned me for months before sending me to Ravensbrück. On the third day of my stay in Ravensbrück, my Communist fellow prisoners subjected me to a third degree. They knew that I was Heinz Neumann's companion and that I had made no secret of our bitter experience in the Soviet Union. When they were through, they claimed I had been spreading lies about the Soviet Union and branded me a traitor. As the Communist women enjoyed considerable prestige among the inmates, their ostracism had the desired effect; from then on, my fellow politicals made a point of avoiding me.

Milena Jesenská was the first among the political prisoners who not only spoke to me but showed that she trusted me. I was thankful for having been sent to Ravensbrück, because it was there I had met Milena.

Ravensbrück is in Mecklenburg, fifty miles north of Berlin. In 1940 the Gestapo interned five thousand women there, political offenders, Jews, members of proscribed religious groups, Gypsies, criminals, and so-called asocials. By the end of the war there were roughly twenty-five thousand women in the camp. At first there were sixteen ground-level barracks. Others were built little by little, and in the end there were thirty-two. Apart from the criminals and asocials, the prisoners were from all walks of life. They differed widely from one another, but all in all they were very much like women at freedom. With the exception of the German, Polish, and Czech politicals and the Jehovah's Witnesses, there were relatively few conscious political oppositionists at the start. Later on, their numbers were swelled by

3

members of the resistance movements in all the countries occupied by Hitler.

The politicals found it easier than others to adapt to conditions in the camp. Their being sent to a camp proved they were regarded as a threat to National Socialism, and that increased their self-respect. But most of the inmates were harmless innocents who had no idea why they had been sent to that ghastly place or for how long.

Every one of these women lived in thoughts of the life she had been wrenched away from, of her children, her husband, her parents. And now they were drilled like recruits and hadn't a minute of the day or night to themselves. At every step they were surrounded by others as unhappy as themselves. In every barracks an individual might be attracted to one or two others, but she was sure to find the vast majority unbearable in every way. The SS members, of both sexes, who ran the camp saw to it that the inmates were permanently cold and hungry, worked them like dogs, and even beat them.

The loss of liberty alone can bring about drastic character changes. But when the constant fear of death is added to the daily torments of prison life, the shock is so great that most prisoners cease to react normally. Some, in self-defense, become appallingly aggressive; others cringe and crawl, and still others give way to a despondency that undermines their defenses against sickness or death.

In the course of his or her confinement, every prisoner must go through different stages. One of the gravest dangers is inability to surmount the first shock of arrival at the camp. To survive, the prisoner had somehow to adapt to this extreme situation and give meaning to the new life, terrible as it was. Only a few succeeded by a great effort of the will in finding a new balance. Though ill on her arrival, Milena was one of these. Even in the first bewildering days of her stay, she took a keen

4

interest in her fellow prisoners. In other words, she kept her grip on life.

The new arrivals were housed in special barracks and took their daily "exercise" separately from the others. Though this was strictly forbidden, I was able to join them every day, because, as *Blockälteste* of the Jehovah's Witnesses barracks, I wore a green armband, which gave me a certain freedom of movement in the camp. Every day Milena waited for me by the Wailing Wall. I knew what the newcomers went through during their first weeks, when the horrors were still new. But Milena never wasted a single word on her own suffering. As a journalist she was interested first and foremost in what others said and did. I have never met another reporter so utterly devoted to her calling. She was wonderfully skilled at asking questions; with her opening words, a rapport was established. In her interviews she never played a role or hid behind a mask. In every interview she created an atmosphere of intimacy, because she invariably identified with the person she was questioning. She had a remarkable gift of empathy.

When questioning me about my experience in Soviet Russia, she no longer seemed to be living in the present. Her imagination threw her back into the past, and she was able to flesh out my memory of things I had long forgotten. She was not content to hear about events; she wanted to *see* the people I had met on my long march through the Soviet prisons, to know all about them, their idiosyncrasies, their way of speaking; she even wanted to hear the songs they had sung in those faraway camps. Her manner of questioning was a creative act; it enabled me for the first time to give form to my recollections.

Day after day, in installments, I supplied her with a chronological record of my experiences in the Soviet Union. But that wasn't enough for her. She also questioned me about my political past. Once she interrupted me with the question: "Tell me, how long did you believe in the Communist party? How long did you believe that the party and the Comintern were really trying to bring about a political and economic order that would guarantee work, bread, and freedom to all?" Searching my memory, I soon recalled the days of my first occasional doubts, which my craving for political certainty had always repressed. We agreed (for Milena, too, had been taken in for a time by the Communist message) that Communists are extraordinarily fruitful in inventing excuses for the obvious failings of their party, for its betrayals of its original program. We agreed that it takes an enormous shock to open their eyes to the party's opportunism and hypocrisy and give them the strength to break with it. Together we began to examine the roots of the Communist evil.

Milena herself had never been in the Soviet Union. But the events of 1936 and the first of the Moscow show trials had led her to tear up her party card. From then on, as a journalist, she followed the horrors of the Great Purge behind the Iron Curtain attentively. In an article about the lies broadcast by Radio Moscow, she had addressed the following questions to the leadership of the Russian party: ". . . We would like to know what has become of the many Czech Communists and plain workers who went to Soviet Russia years ago . . . Is it not true that the greater part of them are in your prisons? For," she went on, "that is how the Soviets treat the people who were foolish enough to believe that they, as Communists, were under Soviet protection. . . ." And taking up the sad fate of the German Communist refugees in Czechoslovakia, she concluded her article with the sentence: "Among them [the Communist refugees] are people whom I greatly esteem and others whom I utterly despise. But whatever my personal dislike, I would never go so far as to wish any of them to be 'welcomed' into the workers' fatherland."*

---

*Milena Jesenská, "Good Advice Is Worth Its Weight in Gold," *Přítomnost* (*The Present*), March 8, 1939.

Still, her knowledge of the inhuman conditions prevailing in the "workers' fatherland" was purely theoretical, and I well understood the excitement with which she listened to my report. That was in 1940. In those days hardly anything was known in the West about the mass arrests and the slave camps in Russia. Milena was quick to understand the importance of my testimony. I believe we had known each other for just a week when she announced, "When we are free again, let's write a book together." She had in mind a book about the concentration camps of both dictatorships, the roll calls, the marching uniformed columns, the millions of human beings reduced to slavery; in the one, dictatorship in the name of socialism; in the other, for the profit and glory of the master race.

The title was to be "The Age of the Concentration Camps." Her suggestion left me stunned. What! Me collaborate on a book? What could she be thinking? I was incapable of writing a single line. But Milena was too full of our project to notice my distress. Then and there she told me how she pictured our collaboration. "You'll write the first part, everything you've been telling me; the second part will be about our life in Ravensbrück; we'll write that together. . . ." When I got my voice back and objected feebly that I was incapable of writing, she gently took hold of my nose as if I were a puppy, and said, "But, Gretushka, anyone who can tell a story as well as you can write. It's much worse for me. I can hardly describe someone coming into a room. Besides, you ought to know that anyone who's not totally illiterate can write. Your Prussian schooling has ruined you. Those essays they make you write."

For someone born and bred in Potsdam like me, it's not easy to speak of feelings, of love and grief and great happiness. Milena had no such inhibitions. She laughed at me, her "little Prussian." She often spoke of herself as a "little Czech," sometimes adding a few hard words about the national character of her people, whom she loved with a painful tenderness. She never showed the slightest trace of the nationalism and xenophobia so common among the inmates of all nationalities.

Milena, who never hesitated to ask questions, soon learned of my deep sorrow. She began to talk about Heinz Neumann and wanted to know what sort of man he was. When she asked me, "Did you love him very much?" I was too choked with tears to answer. Three years had passed since Heinz was taken away by the NKVD in Moscow. I had been tortured by nightmares ever since. I was sure he was dead and had given up hope of ever seeing him again. Now Milena reopened the wound. I was overwhelmed by the despair I had fought so hard to overcome. To comfort someone, one must be able to experience his suffering, and that is a rare gift. In helping me to recover, Milena found the way to my heart.

Every time we met I was horrified by Milena's pallor and her swollen hands. I knew she was in pain, I knew how she suffered from the cold during the interminable daily roll calls, and under the thin blankets at night. But if ever I mentioned her sufferings, she laughed and changed the subject. In 1940 she still seemed totally unbroken, full of courage and energy. Her great spirit still triumphed over her weak body.

It was plain to me that she suffered from hunger, though she never said a word about it. I knew only too well what it was to be hungry, so one day, unable to bear it any longer, I brought her my bread ration. She pushed it away with an air of annoyance, which puzzled me at the time. She explained much later. The mere thought of accepting bread from me made her miserable, because in our friendship she always wanted to be the giver. She wanted to help me and care for me. When I told her I had a family, a mother and brothers and sisters, she seemed disappointed. She wanted me to be all alone in the world, wholly dependent on her care and help. To her, friendship meant doing everything, sacrificing everything for another.

———

Everything Milena did was a protest against the camp regime. She didn't march right in rows of five, she didn't stand right at roll call, she didn't hurry when ordered to, she didn't toady to those in command. Every word Milena said was an infringement of the regulations. While, surprisingly enough, the SS personnel were intimidated by her intellectual superiority, her behavior infuriated the other political prisoners, most of all the Communists with their mania for discipline. I remember a roll call one spring evening. The trees behind the camp wall were just beginning to turn green. A soft, fragrant breeze was blowing from that direction. There wasn't a sound to be heard. Milena must have forgotten all about camps and roll calls; perhaps she was dreaming of some park in the suburbs of Prague, where the crocuses were coming up through the grass. She began to whistle a tune. The Communists who were standing all around her exploded with indignation. "It's easy for them," said Milena in telling me about it, "they were born to be prisoners; they have discipline in their bones."

Another time she was marching along the camp street with a detail on the way to work. I was standing by the side of the street, waiting to nod to her. Catching sight of me, she tore off her regulation headscarf and waved to me over the heads of the horrified prisoners and the amazed SS guards.

But the Communist women's hatred of Milena had still other causes. The Czech Communists had frowned on our friendship from the start of our brief meetings. I had told Milena about the third degree the German Communists had put me through, and I was afraid something of the kind would happen to her. I was very much surprised when she told me that in spite of her break with the party the Czech Communists, far from treating her as a traitor, curried favor with and even found her light work in the camp infirmary. This they were able to do, because the SS management of the camp made things easy for themselves by entrusting the internal administration to the inmates. In most other camps, this internal administration was dominated by the criminal element, but here in Ravensbrück the politicals were put in charge. The SS appointed messengers, *Blockälteste*, assignment clerks, orderly room clerks, nurses, later even doctors, and of course the camp police. Inmates holding these "posts," as they were called, became a class by themselves, intermediate between the SS authorities and the mass of slave laborers. In such positions they were able to help their fellow inmates very considerably, and many did all they could to mitigate the hardships of camp life, but others made common cause with the SS oppressors, and I am sorry to say that this was not unusual. Since the number of inmates increased steadily, the SS were always having to appoint more prisoners to administrative posts, and were open to suggestions from the inmates, who of course knew a lot more than the SS did about the qualifications of their fellow prisoners. It goes without saying that the Communist women reserved the good jobs almost exclusively for their comrades. Which makes it all the more surprising that they should help a political enemy—one more proof of the power of Milena's personality.

But Milena's friendship with me went too far for the comrades. Their spokeswomen Palečková and Ilse Machová approached her. Did she know I was a Trotskyist, who was spreading infamous lies about the Soviet Union? Milena listened to their outburst of hatred and replied that she had had ample opportunity to form her own opinion of my reports on the Soviet Union and saw no reason to doubt their credibility. Soon after this warning, the Communists presented Milena with an ultimatum: She would have to choose between membership in the Czech community in Ravensbrück and friendship with the German Buber-Neumann. Milena made her choice, in full awareness of the consequences. After that the Communist women persecuted her as hatefully as they did me.

2

STRONGER THAN ANY BARBARISM

. . . and this is another instance of your life-giving power, Mother Milena . . .

—FRANZ KAFKA, *BRIEFE AN MILENA*

Deep friendship is always a great gift. But if such good fortune is experienced in the desolation of a concentration camp, it can become the content of a life. During our time together Milena and I succeeded in defeating the unbearable reality. And because it was so strong, because it filled our whole beings, our friendship became something more, an open protest against the humiliations imposed on us. The SS could prohibit everything, they could treat us like disembodied numbers, threaten us with death, enslave us—in our feeling for each other we remained free and unassailable. It was toward the end of November, during our evening exercise, that we dared for the first time to walk arm in arm. This was strictly forbidden in Ravensbrück. It was dark, and we walked in silence, with strangely long steps as though dancing, peering into the milky moonlight. Not a breath of wind. Somewhere far away, far from our world, the wooden clogs of the other inmates shuffled and crunched. For me nothing existed but Milena's hand on my arm and the wish that this walk might never end. And then the siren howled: Time to turn in. All the others ran to their barracks. But we hesitated, holding each other tight, unwilling to part. The bellowing voice of an overseer came closer. Milena whispered, "Come to the Wailing Wall later. So we can be alone for just a few minutes." Then we parted. Someone shouted, "Damn bitches!" That was us.

At the appointed time I slipped away from the bustling crowd in the barracks. It didn't even occur to me that this meeting might end with a flogging or solitary confinement or even death. It didn't cross my mind that someone might see me. I ran past the lighted windows, came to the path beside the Wailing Wall. It was pitch-dark and I couldn't see a thing. To muffle the sound of my wooden clogs, I groped my way to the edge of the path and continued on the grass. I saw something bright behind the leafless bushes that bordered the windowless wall of the second barracks. In my haste and excitement I tripped over a stump and fell into Milena's arms.

Next morning, as usual, the roll call was interminable. Sometimes, because of her work at the infirmary, Milena was exempted. The three hundred occupants of my barracks were standing motionless and silent on the camp street, across from the infirmary, waiting for the SS duty officer to come and call the roll. I saw Milena in the corridor of the infirmary. She stepped up to a closed window, looked at me, laid one hand on the windowpane and moved it slowly back and forth in a silent, affectionate greeting. I was overjoyed. I nodded to her. Suddenly I felt terribly afraid for her. Hundreds of eyes must have seen what I saw. An SS guard might turn up at any moment. The long corridor had six or seven windows, and at each one Milena calmly repeated her loving gesture.

Because of her work in the infirmary, Milena was automatically assigned to No. 1 Barracks, the best in the camp, that of the "old" politicals, interned for their "subversive opinions." One of its main advantages was that it was less crowded than the other barracks. At that time, as I've already said, I was *Blockälteste* of Barracks No. 3, that of the Jehovah's Witnesses. Each barracks had an orderly room for the SS overseer, to which the *Blockälteste* also had access. It was the only room in which a certain privacy was possible. The SS overseer spent a few hours a day there, but at night the room was empty.

Sometimes Milena risked coming to see me, when she knew the SS overseer wouldn't be there. As she was employed in the infirmary, she was able to enter the barracks during working hours on various errands. When that happened, I took her to the orderly room, and we were able to talk for a few minutes undisturbed. But that too was dangerous; the overseer was a permanent threat.

Our longing to spend more time together became more and more imperious. One evening during exercise period—it was autumn by then, and the nights were dark and stormy—Milena informed me of her plan. Half an hour after the SS guards made their night round, she would climb out of her barracks window and cross the camp street—where trained wolfhounds were let loose at night—to mine. I was to open the window for her. At the thought of the terrible danger she would be incurring, my heart skipped a beat. But her determination shamed me, and I agreed. Half an hour after the night round, I opened my barracks door and listened. I couldn't see my hand before my face and it was pouring rain. As I listened for footsteps, my tense nerves made me hear menacing sounds on all sides: SS boots crunching on gravel, shots on the camp street. But this was a time of great activity in the barracks, and I had to avoid being seen. Every few minutes one of the three hundred occupants would go to the toilet, and then I had to hurry away from my listening post.

Suddenly the door was opened from the outside, and in stepped Milena, whistling softly *It's a long way to Tipperary, it's a long way to go* . . . I seized her by the arm and pulled her into the orderly room.

Her hair was dripping, the slippers she had put on to avoid making noise were soaked through. But what did it matter? She had made it. We sat down by the warm stove, which I had lit beforehand, and felt as if we had escaped from jail. We would be free for a whole night.

The dark, warm room gave us a sheltered feeling. Milena crept close to the stove to dry. "Your hair smells like a baby's," I whispered, laughing. And a little later: "Please, Milena, won't you tell me about your home in Prague, when you were little. What you looked like. . . ." Up until then Milena had told me very little about her life. But that November night, all by ourselves, as though safe on an island, I got her to talk.

Milena was born in Prague in 1896, and her earliest memories took her back before the turn of the century. Her mother was a beautiful woman with wavy chestnut-brown hair. In the morning, she often sat at the mirror in a long, soft dressing gown, combing her hair. "This is where she always kissed me." Milena took my hand and put it on her hair. "Here, on this cowlick. I'll never forget it. . . ." Until she was three, she was the only child in the family. She spent her days in the large apartment with the dark furniture. She wasn't taken out very often. Mornings she sat in the dining room, and afternoons in the living room. She sat on high chairs at the high table, with her favorite toys spread out in front of her. "Were you, too, as a child, so fascinated by glass marbles with colored veins?" Milena asked me. "Did you think they were something absolutely magical?" We got to talking about bright-colored Bohemian glass beads, about the miracle of swift mountain streams, and I had difficulty in bringing her back to her childhood. "What did you look like when you were three? Are there any pictures of you at that age?" "Very pale and delicate, with precocious, defiant eyes in a little round face and a tousled mop of hair. I was neither a beautiful child nor a good one. In fact, I behaved very badly. My mother was the only one who really understood me. . . ."

Milena's mother, who died young, came of a well-to-do Czech family, the owners of Bad Beloves, a spa near Náchod. Milena was often taken there as a child. Her mother's family did not, like her father's, belong to the old, established bourgeoisie, but had gradually worked their way up the social ladder. Czech families like hers were distinguished by their enormous respect for every branch of culture, for science, art, the theater, and music, and they played a large part in the recent awakening of the Czech national consciousness.

Milena's mother was thought to be "artistic." In keeping with the taste of the day, she did peasant-style wood carvings, poker work, and furniture with rustic ornaments. Milena remembered that in her parents' apartment which, like most homes of the wealthy Prague bourgeoisie, was full of imitation-Renaissance furniture, there was a chair that her mother herself had turned and carved, an extraordinary piece, with a triangular, leather-upholstered seat and a knob at the front, which the child could hold on to while sitting there. Her mother also favored colored peasant headscarves, and later on, when Milena began to travel on her own, there would always be a few of these scarves in her luggage. She would spread them out to give her hotel rooms a personal touch.

But even as a little girl Milena had had entirely different tastes from her mother's. She remembered an incident that had made her weep. "That was when my mother took away the little pink-and-blue combs I had brought home from some parish fair and given me one made of genuine tortoiseshell, that I didn't like at all. I also remember that my sailor's blouse drove me crazy; I wanted one with lace and ribbons like the one Fanda, who lived next door, had. . . ."*

*Milena Jesenská, *The Way to Simplicity* (Prague, 1926).

15

"But I want you to know one thing," said Milena sadly. "My mother never spanked me when I was little. She never even scolded me. Only my father did that. . . ."

She was shivering. She was cold and tired. The stove had gone out and the sounds of a new day in camp came in to us. Our time together was drawing to an end.

3

JAN JESENSKY

The Jesenskys lived on the sixth floor of a house in the center of Prague. "The Příkopě and Václavské Náměstí [Wenceslaus Square] were right under our windows," Milena began. "In those days there were still beautiful low buildings around there, dating from the late baroque period. The whole neighborhood looked like a small provincial town with its neat central square.

"The tension between the Czechs and the German-speaking Austrians took many different forms. One of them could be seen from our windows every Sunday morning. The Austrian students with their bright-colored caps would stroll on the right side of the Příkopě and the Czechs in their Sunday best would promenade on the left side. Now and then a crowd would form, people would start singing something or other, and you could feel the exasperation in the air. I saw all that from the window, but I didn't really know what it was all about.

"Then came a Sunday that I'll never forget. I saw the Austrian students come marching from the Powder Tower, not as usual on the sidewalk, but in the middle of the street. They were marching in formation and singing. Suddenly a crowd of Czechs appeared from Václavské Náměstí; they too were marching in the middle of the street, but silently. My mother and I were standing at the window. She held me by the hand, a little more tightly than necessary. As the Czechs advanced, I saw my father in the front ranks. I recognized him right away, and I was delighted to see him down there, but my mother was pale and tense. Suddenly a detachment of police came rushing out of Havírská ulice and placed themselves between the two hostile armies, cutting off both from the Příkopě. But both sides continued to advance. The Czechs reached the police cordon and were ordered to halt; then a second time they were ordered to halt, then a third time. . . . I don't remember exactly what happened then. I only know that I heard shots and saw the peaceful crowd of Czechs transformed into a howling mob. Suddenly the Příkopě was deserted. Only one man stood facing the police rifles—my father. I can still see him standing calmly there with his hands at his sides. But beside him on the cobblestones lay something strange and horrible. I don't know if you've ever seen what someone looks like who has been shot and crumples. He's not human anymore, he looks like an old rag. My father probably didn't stand there for more than a minute. It seemed years to my mother and me. Then he bent down and began to bandage the bundle of human flesh. My mother had closed her eyes and two big tears were rolling down her cheeks. I still remember that she took me in her arms and squeezed me as if she had wanted to crush me. . . ."*

Milena's father played a larger part in her recollections than her mother. All the experiences that marked her most deeply were connected with her father, whom she both loved and hated. And this to the end of her life.

Dr. Jan Jesensky was a professor at the Charles University in Prague and practiced dentistry on Ferdinand Street, one of the most fashionable streets in Prague. He came of an old but impoverished middle-class family, and had grown wealthy by working hard at his profession. He was regarded as an outstanding oral surgeon and founded a school that still bears his name.

*Milena Jesenská, "On the Art of Standing Still," *Přítomnost*, April 5, 1939.

Milena looked very much like her father; she had the same dimple on her chin and the same resolute mouth. They were also both strong-willed, unyielding.

Jan Jesensky taught his only child old-fashioned patriarchal manners. She had to kiss his hand in greeting and in speaking to him was not allowed to use the familiar form of address.

Dr. Jesensky was proud of his achievements and determined to play a leading role in the Czech society of Prague. Anything that might interfere with this, especially his family, had to give way.

Undoubtedly Milena's love-hate for her father had its roots in her early childhood. When she was about three, a son was born to the Jesenskys. Without knowing it, the sensitive little girl must have sensed what this new child meant to her father and mother. It was a boy and she was only a girl. She would stand behind the door and listen anxiously to the sickly baby's screams. Sensing her parents' anxiety, she too trembled for the baby's life. When he died, she thought her parents had loved only him. How much his death had meant to her can be judged by the fact that Franz Kafka in his love letters to Milena speaks of her little brother's grave, which he visited.

Her father often spanked her when she had been naughty or obstinate. But once he threw her into a big chest full of dirty washing and left the lid closed over the screaming child until she thought she would smother. From then on she lived in terror of her father.

Jan had a ferocious temper; in his frequent fits of rage he shouted threats and obscenities. He did his tyrannical best to break Milena's spirit and force his opinions on her. In public he posed as an ultraconservative eccentric. He dressed in the old-fashioned style of a provincial nobleman, and never went out without a frock coat and the low-crowned top hat that went with it. He got up at four in the morning and took a cold bath; by half-past five he could be seen in the Kinsky Gardens, wearing

19

his monocle and accompanied by two big dogs. He took his afternoon nap not on a soft couch, but on a hard, old-fashioned sofa. And he never failed to mention his Spartan virtues as a means of impressing, if not seducing, the ladies. In the afternoon he appeared, every inch the Herr Professor, in his elegantly appointed dentist's office. Jan Jesensky was an unfortunate mixture of great ability and dishonest, brutal egoism. Every evening he went to his club and lost hundreds of crowns at cards.

In Ravensbrück we were allowed to write letters. The writing paper, which we had to buy at the canteen, carried the letterhead—Ravensbrück Concentration Camp—and just below it the regulations governing the inmates' correspondence with the outside world. There were different kinds of paper for different categories of inmate. The "old" politicals, who had been arrested before the war, were allowed to write sixteen lines twice a month, and on their paper the letterhead and regulations were printed in red. In addition to the usual regulations, the Jehovah's Witnesses' paper, printed in green, had the words: "I am still a Jehovah's Witness"; they were allowed to write only five lines. All those arrested during the war had a black letterhead; they were allowed to write sixteen lines but only once a month, and the replies of their correspondents were limited to sixteen lines.

Once in 1942, the mail distribution brought on an outburst of grief. There were hundreds of Gypsies in Ravensbrück, classified as "asocial" and "racially inferior." In 1941 a so-called family camp for Gypsies was set up near the Auschwitz death camp. Whole tribes of Gypsies lived there, men, women, and children, deprived of their freedom but living in a relatively mild form of captivity. Later on, the families were torn apart; men, women, and children were transferred to regular concentration camps. The extermination of the Gypsies must have begun at the end of 1942, and this is how we got news of it in Ravensbrück. Soon after the mail was handed out, women came

20

running out of the Gypsies' barracks, screaming and holding up the letters they had just received. Nearly all contained the same notification, that a husband, a son, or a brother had "died in the hospital." The women howled with grief, tore their clothes, and beat their faces in an Oriental outburst of despair that swept away all camp discipline. From then on the mail was censored more strictly than ever.

Even so, the inmates waited impatiently for Saturday, when the mail was distributed. The 150 words a month we were allowed to receive in the first years were our only contact with our dear ones outside. The mere sight of a familiar handwriting brought comfort, but despair as well. What tears were shed over these letters!

Milena exchanged one letter a month with her father. Every letter she received from him churned up the whole past and aroused new antagonisms. Still, she tried to be fair to her father.

At Christmas 1941 the camp management had a sudden burst of humanitarian sentiment. For the first time the inmates' relatives were authorized to send packages, though of specified weight and contents. Most surprisingly, each package could include a woolen jacket.

I ran to Milena with my package. I had opened it, and a golden-yellow knitted jacket lay on top. I was beside myself with pleasure, and I wondered why she was reluctant to show me hers. Her father had sent her a Bavarian costume jacket, and she was ashamed of his bad taste. I did my best to comfort her and asked how she had dressed "before." But that was another sore point. A severe illness had caused her to put on so much weight that she lost all interest in clothes. But now that she was as slim as she had been as a young girl, she felt quite differently. She forgot the silly costume jacket and we reveled in fantasies about the lovely clothes we would wear "later." Milena saw herself in a tailored suit; she had always looked well in tailored suits.

An early photo of Milena shows her on the banks of the Vltava, wearing a striped two-piece suit with a long pleated skirt, a tam, and high laced shoes. She is holding a chic little umbrella. All very elegant and in the taste of the time. Her soft, childlike profile, her Czech snub nose, and her luxuriant hair stand out against a light background. She must have been about thirteen when the picture was taken. Her mother, who was then still alive, had Milena's clothes made by a dressmaker.

"When I was about fourteen, I was sent my first flowers, a real bouquet from Dietrich's flower shop. They came with a visiting card, addressing me as 'Miss'! There it was for all the world to see. The flowers had been sent by my first admirer, as a result, so to speak, of my first kiss. Shall I tell you about it? It's a rather sad story, I still can't think of it without a pang. Councilor Matuš was a friend of my father's, a great skier and sportsman. He suffered from cataract. For months he was in danger of going blind. He was a man of the old school, a bachelor, a famous waltzer, honorable, upright, courageous, and not at all calculating, either in love or in money matters. In short, a gentleman such as you don't see anymore. When I visited him in the hospital, I brought him a bunch of violets. They took me to his room. I saw that his eyes were bandaged and realized that he had to spend whole days inactive in a darkened room, not knowing whether he would ever see again. I felt ashamed of my thoughtlessness in bringing him violets which he couldn't even see, and the feel of which would only remind him of his misfortune. I wanted terribly to undo the harm I had done, to make him a present that would give him pleasure even if he couldn't see it. So I threw my arms around him and kissed him. It was the first kiss of my life and I didn't like it at all, because he needed a shave and I was so excited that my kiss landed on his nose and slid down to his chin. Once it was done, I tried to explain, but I didn't know what to say. The best I could do was stammer idiotically, 'That's not what I meant,' though I had no idea what he was thinking or what I might have meant. I was so confused that baby tears came to my eyes. But when I got home, a bouquet of magnificent hothouse lilacs was waiting for me with a visiting card, addressing me as 'Miss,' followed by a few words—something about the 'best possible present' for a sick man, proving that he knew perfectly well what I had meant. And my father said, 'You see? Now there's a gentleman.' "*

Jan Jesensky, who was always dressed fit to kill and looked much younger than his age, once spent a few days with this Councilor Matuš in his summer house outside of Prague. Both men were fifty at the time. Matuš looked sadly at the landscape and said with a sigh: "For fifty years I've been looking at these trees. One year is like another, nothing ages as much as we do. Always the same budding, flowering, and fading . . ." Such world-weariness was beyond Jesensky. He replied: "These trees. I've *only* been looking at them for fifty years. Every year they look new to me and they always will."

Milena's mother had been ill with pernicious anemia for years. If only for educational reasons, Dr. Jesensky thought it advisable that his daughter should help care for the invalid. Though only thirteen, Milena would stay with her mother until her father came home—often after nightfall—and relieved her. Milena's mother sat up in bed, propped on pillows, while Milena in her chair struggled to keep awake. Every time her mother's head drooped, Milena would start up guiltily, for she had fallen asleep. She would hurry over to the bed and help her mother up. But a few minutes later the same thing would happen again. At length her father came home from his card game or his lady friends, often in a state of euphoria. He would try to cheer the patient up with jokes and amusing stories, but it seemed to Milena that this only offended her and made her more aware of

*Milena Jesenská, *The Way to Simplicity*.

23

her pitiful condition. Milena loved her mother dearly, but now her strength failed her, she lost control over her nerves. One day, when nothing she did could satisfy the patient, she lost her temper and threw a tray with a whole meal on it on the floor. These were difficult days for the mother and the little girl. Her mother's sufferings were such agony to Milena that she was almost relieved when at last death came.

Milena was thirteen when her mother died. Suddenly she found herself independent, free to dispose of her time, abandoned to her own resources. She describes herself as an emotional teenager, at once sentimental and rebellious. Once she took a room in a third-class hotel and stayed there all night by herself. It was an exciting adventure. It gave her a delightful feeling of being grown up, and besides, she hoped to find out what mysterious thing went on in these ill-famed hotels. She spent the night in a whirl of erotic imaginings, but nothing happened.

This was not her only nocturnal adventure. The cemetery had a magical attraction for her. She would sit on the wall, looking at the graves, and bask in tearful weltschmerz.

There were violent scenes when her father learned of her escapades, but the more he fumed, the more liberties she took. She had plenty of opportunity. As no one checked to see if she came home at night, she went right on with her adventures, triumphantly flouting her father's authority. The painter Scheiner asked her to pose for his illustrations of fairy tales, and through him, while hardly more than a child, she became acquainted with a group of ultraconservative painters that called itself "Jednota." Her experiences in their studios gave her a profound shock, and she recalled this period with loathing. Speaking of her father, or rather, of all parents, she once said, "Irresponsibly, they bring children into the world and, hardly bothering to get acquainted with them, push them out into life: 'All right, now you can take care of yourself.'"

At fifteen Milena seemed an adult to all who knew her. She had matured; mentally as well as physically, she had lost her girlish qualities and become a young woman. She had the unusual gift of being able to meet adults on their own ground. No doubt her conflict with her father, from whose influence she was determined to free herself, had a good deal to do with her precocity.

At that time Milena was a passionate reader, mainly of novels by Knut Hamsun, Dostoevsky, George Meredith, Tolstoy, J. P. Jacobsen, Thomas Mann, and others. It is hard to say what enabled her at so early an age to find herself and develop a sense of values. In her home she found nothing to guide her; she had only her own burgeoning mind, which led her to reject everything base, sordid, or in bad taste. Her conflict with her father had a profound effect on her that would take her years to surmount. In her rebellion against the conventional pseudomorality she had come to despise, she overshot the mark and lost all sense of proportion. Why should she let others tell her what was right and wrong, true and untrue? She would decide for herself. At that time she was widely regarded as a liar. But her critics failed to see that she, like many young rebels, was in a transitional stage, trying to work out her own standards. Her insecurity expressed itself in a dangerous arrogance, and she went through a period of moral collapse, from which, however, she was to make an admirable recovery.

4

THE MINERVANS
COME OF AGE

Milena attended the Minerva School for Girls, which maintained the high educational standards of the old Austrian Empire. Latin and Greek were compulsory. One of the earliest secondary schools for girls, it had been founded at considerable financial sacrifice by a small group of Czech intellectuals. Its students included many who became prominent Czech teachers, sociologists, and physicians. Dr. Alice Masaryk, daughter of Tomáš G. Masaryk, the founder and subsequent president of the Czechoslovakian Republic, was among the first graduates.

Milena and her emancipated school friends were often referred to, half admiringly, half ironically, as "the Minervans." Though an excellent student, Milena was far from being a model child. Close friendships were formed, not only, as usual, among members of the same school class, but also, in a manner of speaking, "vertically." Members of different classes having the same interests and abilities were drawn together, a case in point being the trio: Milena—Staša—Jarmila. Milena influenced the other two in very different ways, and meant something very different to each of them. Jarmila was so smitten with Milena that she took to imitating her almost slavishly. She wore the same clothes, made by the same dressmaker and paid for by Dr. Jesensky, though he didn't know it. She spoke in the same tone of voice as Milena, affected the same facial expression and the same gliding movements. There was a strong physical resemblance between the two girls—they had the same beautiful figure, the same slender waist, and fine, long legs; both had magnificent hair—and this may have given Jarmila the idea of aping her friend. But Jarmila went even further. She even managed to imitate Milena's expressive and highly original handwriting. Though she was well aware of what she was doing, it was quite innocent and merely showed how very much she admired her friend. She read the same books as Milena, listened to the same music, and fell in love with anyone Milena happened to be in love with. But to her great disappointment she always remained a few steps behind her idol. And that is not to be wondered at, for Apollo's breath had never touched her; there was nothing Dionysian about Jarmila.

With Staša, who was two years younger, it was a very different matter. The grown-ups referred to Staša and Milena as "the Siamese Twins," and whispered that they were lesbians. Actually, it was the sort of infatuation that can exist only between sixteen-year-old girls. Both were in a state of ecstasy, totally wrapped up in each other. But there was nothing physical, nothing erotic, about their love. Nor were they jealous of each other; there was no possessiveness, only an empathy free from unkindness, a tenderness that never lost its innocence. Staša deliberately denied herself the right to criticize her friend and never hesitated to do whatever Milena, her superior, wanted. And yet, unlike Jarmila, she never sacrificed her own strong personality so far as to imitate Milena. She never became Milena's shadow. These girls were full of life, they loved food, delighted in bananas, oranges, chocolate, and whipped cream. Especially bananas, which were then a rarity in Europe.

On the other hand, they sometimes made a show of being as decadent, blasphemous, and morbid as possible. They experimented with medicines that Milena stole from her father's office. They would take all sorts of pills and wait eagerly to see what the effects would be. They even tried cocaine. When warned by adults, they argued that everyone has the right to experiment with his own body.

Dr. Prochaska, Staša's father, despite his reputation for liberalism, was horrified by this friendship between girls. He dramatized it unreasonably and did everything in his power to separate his daughter from Milena, who was indeed responsible for most of their escapades. But in this he was unsuccessful, though he had recourse to drastic methods. In the end, the passionate friendship that had given rise to so much gossip and indignation dwindled away all by itself.

When Milena was graduated from secondary school, her father, wishing her to carry on the medical tradition of the family, made her study medicine. During the First World War he forced her to help him in treating soldiers with face wounds. She was totally unsuited to such work. She was unable to control her nausea and suffered the torments of the wounded men as keenly as if her own face had been torn to pieces. But her father had no patience with such squeamishness. As far as he was concerned, the wounded men were merely "cases," some more interesting than others, which he, as director of the Prague-Žižkov reserve hospital, was called upon to deal with. He experimented and tried to develop new methods of treatment. Milena told me how pleased her father had been with the success of one of his experiments. He had patched up a wounded man, a good part of whose lower jaw had been shot off. But as he had been unable to make the man's salivary glands function normally, he had suspended a rubber bag from the patient's neck for the saliva to drip into. Milena could imagine the life that awaited these poor devils. But Jesensky was proud of his handiwork. He discharged the man as "cured" and sent him home for Christmas. A few days later, a telegram came from the man's parents. Their son had shot himself on Christmas Eve.

After a few terms Milena dropped out of medical school. She tried her hand at music, but though gifted, she didn't get very far; though musical to the fingertips, she did not play very well. In those days it was by no means taken for granted that the daughters of the Prague bourgeoisie should learn a profession. They got married, and in the meantime their fathers supported them. In spite of her emancipation, Milena found it perfectly normal to live at her father's expense, or to put it bluntly, to make free with her father's money. She herself did not live in luxury, she did not have expensive habits. But money flowed through her fingers like water. She made presents, she gave unostentatiously where it was needed or would be enjoyed. No doubt her attitude toward money was one more form of protest against one of the basic tenets of her society, namely, the sanctity of property. In her opinion, anyone who accumulated money for its own sake was inhuman and deserved no consideration.

When I asked about her looks as a young girl, she replied hesitantly, "I didn't think much of them, but other people thought I was beautiful, though not in a classical sense like Staša." A friend, who knew her in her youth, wrote, "Milena was very beautiful, slender, not delicate, but wiry like a boy. The most striking thing about her was her gait; it was never vulgar, she never swayed her hips. That lovely rhythmic gait seemed to cost her no effort at all, she seemed unaware of it. It was not walking, it was a gliding to and fro. You couldn't help seeing how spontaneous it was; her movements were not so much 'graceful' as fluid and immaterial. Her hands were eloquent too; they were rather large with almost bony fingers and expressed her state of mind even more clearly than her words. Her movements were reserved, economical, but that made her slightest gesture all the more expressive. She loved beauty and couldn't live without it. In long, floating robes à la Duncan, with loose hair and an armful of flowers, she was vividly, stirringly beautiful despite her almost exaggerated disregard for what people thought. Milena loved flowers more than anything else; she had a gift for arranging them in a vase with almost Japanese lightness and grace. On flowers she was capable of spending her last groschen, and not always her own. She loved fine clothes but hated overdressing. She was able to devise costumes which, without being fashionable or sexy, were womanly, soft, flowing, and in rich unusual colors. You could say that she dressed her spirit more than her body. Milena loved nature, trees, meadows, water, and sunshine, but she was far from being a nature lover; she wasn't one to investigate nature; she simply needed it in order to live."

Milena was one of those people who spend themselves without stint. But she was far from being unique in her rebellion and wild urge to live. The same was true of other Minervans, especially those who were not markedly intellectual. Ready for any escapades, they gadded about, scandalizing the staid Prague bourgeoisie. This urge to break away from the old social patterns can be explained at least in part by the then prevailing atmosphere in Prague. The whole Czech nation was living in hopeful anticipation of national independence. Prague was a creative center. The young people were avid readers; they devoured the poems of the French symbolists and the Czech "vitalists"; they read Hora, Šrámek, and Neumann as well as the great Russians. In addition, a minority at least of the young Czechs were beginning to form ties with the German and German-Jewish writers living in Prague. National boundaries were giving way. It was a magnificent, though brief, period of intellectual fertility, a period full of expectation and promise.

The writer Josef Kodiček remembered a meeting with Milena in those years: "A sunny scene—I can still see it as clearly as if it were today. Sunday, shortly before noon, on the Příkopě. Prague is still a provincial town. . . . And provincial towns tend to have their corso. The Prague corso was the Příkopě. I see fashionably dressed Germans, I see students promenading, Austrian officers pausing to exchange greetings, smiling, making appointments. On Sunday morning the Příkopě was old-Austrian territory. The commanding figure of Count Thun, the six-foot, eight-inch governor of Prague, towers over the crowd. He's as thin as a stork and the best dressed man on the continent. He stands serenely, in celestial calm, with one foot tucked into the crook of his other knee, surveying the ebb and flow of the crowd through his black-rimmed monocle. Just then two young girls stroll by, arm in arm. They are both something to look at. The first Prague girls to give themselves a deliberately boyish look. Their style is perfect. Their hairdos are modeled on the English Pre-Raphaelites; they are as slender as willow withes, and there is nothing petit bourgeois about their faces or figures. They are probably the first Czech girls of the prewar generation to extend their world from the Czech promenade on Ferdinand Street to the Příkopě corso, thus making contact with the younger generation of German literati. They are genuine European women, a sensation! Count Thun swivels on one leg to look at them, and a wave of enthusiasm and curiosity passes through the crowd. Then Willy Haas, Kornfeld, Fuchs, and a few others of Werfel's circle appear and introduce the two girls to us: Milena and Miss Staša. Clearly, it's Milena who sets the tone.

"Wild stories were told about them: Milena spent money like a drunken sailor; to avoid being late for an appointment, she had swum across the Vltava with her clothes on; she had been arrested in the city park at five o'clock in the morning for picking the 'municipal' magnolias so dear to her lover. Her generosity was as boundless as her extravagance. Bursting with vitality, she burned her candle at both ends.

"To look at them—how shall I put it?—with a somewhat critical eye, there was something stylized, slightly affected about both of them. But how could they have helped it? Those were the days when the Klimt and Preisler period in painting was breathing its last, when the 'Silvery Wind' of the poet Fraňá

Šrámek was blowing over the fields. The Jugendstil of Ružena Svobodova was giving way to a new trend that was a lot more earthy and robust. Young people were beginning to laugh again. Werfel's *Friend of All the World* decreed the joy of living and the brotherhood of man. Decadence was giving way to robust vitality. Werfel was at work on his second volume of poems. A short while later, Milena became the magnetic pole of a whole generation of literary Czechs and Germans, among them a few who had already acquired a European reputation."[*]

Milena felt drawn to German and Jewish intellectuals, not only because they were new to her, but also because among them she encountered an old culture that was very different from the narrow, petty provincialism in which she had grown up. The longing to break away from the Czech culture in which she was still rooted and become a part of a more cosmopolitan movement was characteristic of Milena.

The development of German literature in Prague was an extraordinary phenomenon, for it occurred, as it were, in a vacuum. These German writers had no roots in the country and found no audience among the great mass of Czechs surrounding them. Franz Kafka once wrote to Milena: "I have never lived among the German people. German is my mother tongue and consequently natural to me."[†] This encapsulation in the German language was especially true of the Jewish writers such as Kafka, but also to a lesser degree of the few German writers living in Prague. Of Rainer Maria Rilke, for example. He found no audience among the Czechs, which makes his poetic achievement all the greater. Perhaps it is the encounter between two alien worlds that accounts for the strong mutual attraction between the lively Czech girls and these sensitive writers, an attraction

---

[*]Josef Kodiček, "Radio Free Europe," Munich, broadcast of June 2, 1953.
[†]Franz Kafka, *Briefe an Milena* (*Letters to Milena*) (New York: Schocken Books, 1952), p. 22.

favored as much by the divergence as by the similarities in their ideas, and further encouraged by the fact that all concerned, the Prague Germans and the Czech women, had grown up in the same surroundings, in this city with its ancient streets and bridges and sleepy squares, with its red, gray, and green roofs at the foot of the proud Hradčany castle, in the same Czech landscape, under the same trees, on the gentle banks of the same twining river, the Vltava. In this sharply divided city, they came from very different environments. But now—and this was the new factor—young people on both sides of the divide dropped their deep-seated prejudices and found their way to one another. But for all her interest in new things and people, Milena always remained independent and never imitated anyone. However many Germans and Prague Jews may have attracted her and shared their thoughts with her, she always remained the same warm-hearted, thoroughly Czech girl.

Among the girls at the Minerva School, there were quite a few strong personalities, quite a few shining lights, but Milena outshone them all. What distinguished her most was her strong feeling for others, thanks to which she won the affection of all sorts of people, men as well as women. She recognized no social barriers; she made friends in all walks of life, but she was gifted with a sixth sense that enabled her to detect pretense, to see through the veneer of acquired habits to the heart and core of the human being. Social forms and conventions mattered little to her, least of all those of the narrow bourgeois society in which she had grown up.

The Minervans were in no sense a formal or exclusive group. They never engaged in organized activities on the order of the German Youth Movement. They were all such out-and-out individuals that the mere thought of forming a group would have struck them as absurd. Up until the early thirties, when she joined the Communist party, Milena belonged to no group what-

33

ever, though there were several among the Prague intellectuals. She moved freely among artists and writers of all trends and schools, and was likely to turn up anywhere.

While most of her girlfriends were unduly given to sensual pleasures, Milena, though quite capable of enjoying herself and often accused of amorality, was more intellectual in her ways. The others, the "Bacchantes," regarded her as a kind of blue-stocking.

Milena, the most daring and most anarchistic, was almost the only one who was able, thanks to her energy and vitality, to fulfill the expectations justified by her great gifts. Thanks to some secret force within her, she was able, after sinking to the lowest depths, to rise again and find her way back to normal life and the pursuit of high ambitions.

The young people of those years were molded not only by literature, but also by the feminist movement, which in Bohemia could boast of a particularly romantic tradition. A good friend of Milena once said, "I always thought of her on horseback with a pistol in her belt." He may have been thinking of the "war of the maidens," a legend often invoked by the members of the Bohemian feminist movement. The story is that long, long ago, when Princess Libuša ruled over Bohemia, women were held in high esteem. Wishing to maintain her dynasty, she cast about for a prince consort and chose Přemysl, a simple peasant, sur-named Přemysl the Plowman. When the princess died, Přemysl became ruler over Bohemia, and it was all up with the women's power and prestige. But the women insisted on their old rights and rejected the rule of the new prince and the men. They left Přemysl's castle of Vyšehrad and built one of their own on the Vltava, which they named "Devin," the Maiden's Castle. They then made war on the male sex by force of arms and by guile, but were finally defeated in a decisive battle, in which their leader Vlasta and several hundred maidens lost their lives.

One of the most remarkable Bohemian women and a pioneer

of the feminist movement was the writer Božena Nemcová (1820–1862), whose beautiful book *The Grandmother* is still popular today. Apart from her own writing, she collected and transcribed Czech folktales. Milena has often been likened to her, and in speaking of Milena's style Franz Kafka once said, "In the Czech language I know (with my limited knowledge) only one music, that of Božena Nemcová; here I see a different music, but comparable to the other in determination, passion, tenderness, and above all a clairvoyant intelligence."* There is also a certain similarity in the two women's lives. Both overstepped the bounds of bourgeois morality, both loved with all their hearts, both suffered deep and repeated disappointments, and both subscribed, for a time at least, to the radical political left.

Since Božena Nemcová there have been other outstanding women in Bohemia who have made a name for themselves either in literature or in public affairs. Two of these were Ružena and Marie Jesenská, Milena's aunts and her father's sisters. Marie Jesenská, the younger, was known for her translations of Dickens, George Eliot, and other English novelists. Ružena, the elder, was one of the best-known woman writers of her time. Her early works were sentimental, neoromantic poems, often suggestive of folk songs. Later, she turned to prose, love stories, at which she was more successful. She had the courage to deal with erotic problems, a novelty at the time, especially for a woman writer. She never recovered from her first unhappy love affair. The search for true happiness in love is the main theme of her work. What the well-known Czech literary historian Arne Novak has to say of Ružena Jesenská seems almost to foreshadow the life of her niece. He speaks of her "steadily improving work . . ." and, in connection with her later novels, of "lovingly delineated figures of courageous women who, whether in happiness or in shipwreck, follow only the prompting of their hearts."

---

*Kafka, *Briefe an Milena*, p. 28.

For years Aunt Ružena and Milena disapproved of each other. Horrified at Milena's wild life, her rigidly bourgeois aunt kept trying to mother her. But Milena rebuffed her aunt and made fun of her old-maidishness and sentimental books. Later on, when life had dealt Milena cruel blows, when she had proved herself as a writer and shown political courage as well, mutual respect developed into loving tenderness. Milena fled to Aunt Ružena when in need of comfort and support. In her she found boundless devotion; Ružena loved her despite, or possibly because of, all her faults. Once, when Aunt Ružena was seventy-three years old, she remarked sadly, "I fear I'm growing old; I haven't fallen in love for three years now."

Throughout the history of Bohemia, women distinguished themselves by their courage and combativeness. The same longing for freedom from convention that inspired Milena and the Minervans, the same courage to swim against the stream, runs like a red thread from generation to generation.

Milena may have inherited her spirit of independence. As Jan Jesensky never wearied of pointing out, he was descended from an old Czech family. There is still a memorial tablet in the Old Town Hall listing his ancestor Jan Jessenius among the martyrs of the Czech nation. Born in 1566, Jessenius studied in Breslau, Wittenberg, and Padua, where he took his degree as a doctor of medicine. He then returned to Breslau, became an instructor at the university, and at the same time personal physician to the elector of Saxony. In 1600 he was called to Prague, where the astronomer Tycho Brahe recommended him as physician to the emperor Rudolf II and later to the emperor Matthias.

In Prague, Jan Jessenius soon became a celebrity, both in scientific circles and among the people. In June 1600 he was the first man in Central Europe to dissect a cadaver. In 1617 when a new rector of Charles University was to be elected, the name of Jan Jessenius was put forward. Jessenius, who was a nobleman of Hungarian-Slovak descent, spoke no Czech but only German and Latin, and many thought it inappropriate that a foreigner unversed in the language of the land should be made rector of the Czech university. In the end, however, he was elected, the decisive factor being his Protestantism.

Jessenius fought fearlessly for the progressive ideas of his time, notably freedom of conscience and freedom of scientific investigation, against the opposition of the Church. He resisted the efforts of the emperor Ferdinand II to gain control of the Charles University.

After the "defenestration" of the Catholic councillors in Prague, the revolt of the Bohemian Protestants erupted. Jan Jessenius was among the rebels. After their defeat in the Battle of the White Mountain in 1620, he was arrested along with more than twenty other leaders of the uprising and condemned to death. When the death sentence was read to him, he is quoted as having said, "You are treating us disgracefully, but I want you to know that others will come who will bury with honor our heads, which you will have desecrated and put on show." The manner of his execution was cruel in the extreme; before he was beheaded, his tongue was cut out.

5

THE LOVING ONE

Milena, what a rich, heavy name, almost too full to lift, at first I didn't like it very much, it struck me as a Greek or Roman who had strayed into Bohemia, been brutalized by the Czechs, and cheated out of its accentuation; yet in color and form it is marvelously a woman, whom one carries in one's arms, out of the world, out of the fire, I don't know which, and she nestles willingly and trustingly in one's arms. . . .

—KAFKA, *BRIEFE AN MILENA*

One Sunday the SS man in the guard room was in a good mood and treated us to music. He turned up the volume of the radio and Schubert's *Trout Quintet* came pouring out. We strolled back and forth in delight, surrounded by thousands of women in striped clothes, a promenade of ghosts. Would we ever go to a concert again? Or listen to Mozart? But only too soon we were shaken out of our reverie. In Ravensbrück not even a Sunday stroll was free from perils. Suddenly, a woman overseer rushed in among the strollers and began to beat one of them brutally. What had happened? Two of the inmates had been caught walking arm in arm.

The spell was broken, our enjoyment of sunshine and music was at an end. And to make matters worse, Schubert was replaced by the detested Nazi marches. Our nerves were on edge. I started back to the barracks, but Milena had a better idea, something forbidden, of course. She would go to the infirmary and find the key to the consultation room. No one would think of looking for us there on Sunday. We'd be perfectly safe. She found the key, we opened up and locked ourselves in.

The opaque, rippled windowpanes sparkled like a lake in the sunlight. Sitting side by side on a table with our legs dangling, we forgot the world. When you are condemned to be always in a crowd, it's an enormous pleasure just to be alone in a room. I felt like singing, and I began to hum: *In einem Bächleim helle* . . .

It was then that Milena for the first time called me *člověk boží*. The words are so close to the Russian that of course I knew what they meant. A rough translation might be "divine woman." I was more bewildered than pleased. In all my life I had never been able to conceive of anyone loving, let alone admiring, me. When I asked her what was lovable about me, Milena answered very gravely, "You have the good fortune to love life without reserve. You are as strong and good as the fruitful earth, a little blue village madonna. . . ."

At first I didn't know what attracted me so strongly to Milena; I thought it must be chiefly her intellectual superiority. But soon I realized that what fascinated me most was the aura of mystery surrounding her whole being. Milena did not walk through life with a sure, firm step. She glided. Sometimes, when I saw her from a distance on the camp street, it seemed to me that she had just popped out of nowhere. Even when she was happy, her eyes were always veiled by some bottomless grief. This was no ordinary grief connected with our daily lot; no, it was the grief of one who felt herself to be a stranger in this world, and knew that for her there was no salvation. This evasive, water-nymph-like quality captivated me completely, for I knew I could never get through to her. All my dreams of Milena are haunted by this feeling of hopelessness.

39

Far from ceasing with the loss of freedom, the need for love and affection becomes more imperious than ever. Some of the women in Ravensbrück took refuge in passionate friendships, others eased their heartache by talking endlessly about love, and still others resorted to political or even religious fanaticism.

The passionate friendships of the politicals usually remained platonic, while those of the criminals and asocials often took on a frankly lesbian character. Such relationships, when discovered, were punished with flogging.

In my next to last year at Ravensbrück, when conditions were becoming more and more chaotic, I heard of a lesbian prostitute. Her name was Gerda, but she called herself Gert. She serviced a number of women, but not for money. Every Saturday and Sunday her customers brought her their rations of margarine and sausage, which were distributed only on weekends.

There was also a men's concentration camp at Ravensbrück, but the male and female inmates rarely caught sight of one another. When a column of women on their way to some outside job chanced to pass a group of men, one or the other group would be ordered to halt and about face. They would have to wait with averted eyes until the "temptation" had passed.

Despite the horrors of the camp, the close quarters at which thousands of women were living made for an erotic atmosphere. Once, for example, during the night shift in the SS tailor shop, I heard Gypsy girls, sitting at their sewing machines, sing languorous love songs in spite of the heat, dust, and fatigue. Others worked off their erotic cravings in dance. In the farthermost corner of the stinking latrine, two of them swayed to the languid rhythm of a tango, while their comrades stood guard at the entrance in case the SS should look in.

Love affairs between SS men and inmates were rare. I know of one case in which a German political prisoner working in one of the camp annexes became pregnant; in her despair she committed suicide with sleeping pills obtained at the infirmary.

In No. 1 Tailor Shop, where I worked for a year and a half, an SS man named Jürgeleit and one of the prisoners fell in love with each other. Countless love letters were exchanged, but nothing came of it.

Another such case went further. A young SS man was in charge of a sewing-machine repair shop, where some half a dozen Czech women, including Anička Kvapilová, a friend of Milena's, were working. This SS man—his name was Max Hessler and he was only eighteen—fell in love with one of the Czech girls. They saw each other every day, and his love was as passionate as it was hopeless. In the course of time, he took a great liking to all the Czech women, to the whole Czech nation, in fact. In the end he conceived a daring project—a trip to Prague for his love's sake. He informed his superiors that his sewing machines were in urgent need of certain spare parts, which were available only in Prague. Travel orders were issued and off he went, carrying numerous letters from Czech women to their relatives. In Prague he went from family to family, delivering letters, and the delighted families gave him not only letters but food parcels and other presents for the prisoners. The young lover returned to Ravensbrück with an enormous suitcase, which he somehow managed to smuggle into camp. The letters and presents were distributed. The women were overjoyed and infinitely grateful. But unfortunately too many people were in the know, and Max Hessler's escapades came to the ears of the authorities. He was arrested and some of the women were locked up in the camp prison.

As I later found out, the young man was given a suspended sentence and sent to the front, where he was soon taken prisoner by the French. After the war two former Czech inmates took a trip to France, and went from one POW camp to another until they finally found the brave lover. As a result of their intervention he was soon released.

One gray spring day during working hours, as I was walking along the deserted camp street, I saw a man's shorn head sticking out of a manhole. He had the brutal, crafty face of a hardened criminal. He was looking in the direction of the women's barracks. An "asocial" woman was wriggling her hips in a way that was supposed to be alluring. She had hitched up her dress, a sort of striped sack, well above her calves! And what calves! Her legs were like sticks, covered with blotches. But her posture, her smile, were all feminine coquetry. She had forgotten that starvation had long since ravaged her charms. And her round-headed admirer, leering at her from his manhole, found her desirable.

I described the scene to Milena. She didn't think it funny, but said with a sigh of relief, "Thank God, love is indestructible. It's stronger than any barbarism."

The name Milena means "loving one," and, true enough, her whole life was a story of love and friendship. She first fell in love when she was sixteen. The heroine of a novel she was reading fell in love with a singer, and apparently under its influence Milena fell in love with a singer. His name was Hilbert Vávra. She loved him passionately and without reserve, but the affair proved disappointing. She was too young and Vávra was not the sort of man to bring out her capacity for love. It was not until years later that she encountered a man worthy of her.

One night Milena went to a concert; she was sitting on the steps of the center aisle, immersed in the score. She was wearing a purple evening dress, as though at a royal reception. A man looked over her shoulder and read along with her. The man was Ernst Polak. It was the love of music that first brought them together. Ten years older than she, he was a cultivated man with a profound critical understanding of the arts. In this love affair Milena was to experience supreme happiness and deepest suffering. In a letter to Max Brod, Franz Kafka wrote, "She is living fire, such as I had never seen, a fire, incidentally, that burns only for him [Ernst Polak]. At the same time, extremely affectionate, courageous and intelligent. She puts all that into her sacrifice or, if you prefer, comes by it through sacrifice. But what a man to inspire all this."

The morning after her first night with Ernst Polak, and to complete her happiness, Milena wanted the two of them to watch the sunrise together. Polak, a notorious café dweller, was far from enthusiastic about what he called her crazy idea. But, as he said, "What won't a man do for love?" So in the gray of dawn they climbed one of the hills near Prague, with Polak groaning all the while and complaining about the unaccustomed exertion. Shivering in the cold morning air, he kept asking, "Hasn't it risen far enough?" and making nasty remarks about the "harmful effects of such foolishness."

When Jan Jesensky heard that his daughter was having an affair with Ernst Polak, he flew into a rage and forbade her any further contact with "that Jew." Of course Milena ignored his remonstrances.

Ernst Polak worked as a translator in a Prague bank. But his real interests were elsewhere. He was intimate with numerous writers both in Prague and in Vienna, and acted as a mentor to many of them. Though himself not creative, he had a remarkable feeling for style. He introduced Milena to Franz Kafka, Franz Werfel, and many other writers, including Urzidil, Max Brod, Rudolf Fuchs, and Egon Erwin Kisch. Though very much men of their time, they were largely unpolitical. As they met in the Café Arco in Prague, Karl Kraus, the playwright, in his periodical *Die Fackel* (*The Flame*, spoke of them contemptuously as "Arconauts." He especially had it in for Ernst Polak, and immortalized him as a comic character in one of his plays: *Literature, or Wait and See, a Magical Operetta*, Vienna, 1922.

43

During the First World War, Milena made the acquaintance of Wilma Lövenbach. Their friendship was to last for two decades. Concerning her first meeting with Milena, Wilma was to write: "In midsummer 1916, driving a cabriolet drawn by a little brown horse, I pulled up outside the Hotel Prokop on Mount Špičak, an unpretentious inn at the top of a mountain pass, offering a magnificent view of the woods and meadows of the Bohemian forest. The sun was just setting. To the right and left of the stairs leading up to the inn, I saw two figures that might have been painted by Botticelli, in almost identical flowing robes: Milena and Jarmila. I had long known them by sight; I kept running into them in Prague, on the street or at concerts. I had been struck by their clothes—the goods, the cut, the unusual simplicity, the choice of colors. Milena never wore solid colors. She liked gradations from blue to a cool light gray or to purple and violet. I had heard stories about the two of them from Minervans of my acquaintance. But they spoke almost exclusively of one of them: Milena. Some were critical of her eccentric life style, some envied her, but all admired her." During those weeks at the Prokop, where Professor Jesensky also spent his summer and winter vacations, Wilma and Milena formed a friendship based on their love of poetry. Nineteen sixteen was a great year for Czech poetry; a number of outstanding collections appeared, reflecting no doubt the widespread feeling that national liberation was not far off. For centuries Czech-language literature had either been totally suppressed or hampered in its natural development. Only one art form was able to develop unimpeded in Bohemia. That was the folk song, and it was in folk songs that the poets now sought inspiration. They were the soil from which twentieth-century Czech poetry drew its strength.

The German publisher Franz Pfemfert had commissioned Otto Pick, a Prague journalist and translator, to compile an anthology of German translations of Czech verse for the second issue of his (Pfemfert's) journal *Aktion*. But since Otto Pick had just been drafted into the Austrian army, the writers Jan Lövenbach and Max Brod took over, while Rudolf Fuchs, Pavel Eisner, and Emil Saudek advised them on the choice of material. Wishing to help with the editorial work, Wilma Lövenbach had brought sheafs of Czech verse with her to Mount Špičak. Naturally Milena joined in, and when Ernst Polak turned up one fine day at the neighboring Hotel Rixi, he was drawn into the circle. They sat on the sloping meadows or surrounded by ripening strawberries in the shaded fringe of the forest, reading poem after poem, praising, criticizing, arguing, declaiming, and making their selections. They recited poems by Stanislav K. Neumann, Otakar Fischer, Křička, Šrámek, and Březína. When an unsatisfactory translation called for a new hand, Ernst Polak, who up until then had confined himself to literary theory and criticism, was seized with a passion for translation. Within a few hours he rejoined the others on the meadow with a German translation of Otakar Fischer's "Evening and Soul" and read it to his attentive friends.

One morning Wilma was awakened by a knocking at her door. In came Milena wearing a heliotrope-colored dress and holding a bunch of wildflowers. Her bare feet were wet with the dew of the meadows where she had picked the flowers. She jumped up on Wilma's bed, hugged her, and whispered, "Ernst spent the night with me." She was radiant, utterly exhausted, and entrancingly beautiful.

But the story didn't end there. It became known at the Prokop that Ernst Polak, who was staying at the Rixi next door, which was frequented by Germans and therefore despised by the Czechs, was spending his nights with Milena. Mr. Prokop, an imposing man in his forties, who had known Milena all her life, told her that he wasn't born yesterday, he knew these things happened, but he couldn't allow them in his house, especially not with someone who was staying at the Rixi. Still, because they were old friends, he promised not to tell anyone. Had Milena's father found out, she would have been in trouble, for he had sent her to Mount Špičak to get her away from "that Jew Polak."

A year later, Jan Jesensky, for whom as a Czech patriot Milena's affair with a German Jew was the worst possible disgrace, committed his daughter to a mental home at Veleslavin. He was seconded by Dr. Prochaska, Staša's father who, despite his reputation for kindness and liberalism, was willing to have Milena locked up if that was the only way of "saving" Staša from her influence.

Milena had no suspicion of her father's plan to rob her of her freedom. She had arranged to meet some friends at a bathing establishment on the day when she was taken away by force. Her friends waited in vain, until Alice Gerstl, a close friend of Milena's, came running and told them what had happened.

As was to be expected, Milena suffered unspeakably and resisted at every step. Her impressions of Veleslavin are summed up in a letter she wrote to Max Brod after her release. "You have asked me," she wrote, "to provide some sort of proof that Mr. N. N. is being maltreated in Veleslavin. Unfortunately, I can give you very little definite information that would stand up in court, though I would be very glad to do so. I was in Veleslavin from June 1917 to March 1918; I lived in the same villa, but all I was able to do for him was to lend him books now and then, for which I was locked up several times. He is not allowed to talk to anyone. If it is found out that he has had a conversation, even about the weather and in the presence of a nurse, both parties are locked up and the nurse is dismissed." Max Brod comments: "She goes on to describe the desperate situation in which the inmate found himself. The following sentences many have related to her own experience: 'Psychiatry is a terrible thing when misused. Anything can be interpreted as abnormal, and every word can provide the tormentor with a new weapon. I could swear that there is no good reason why

Herr N. N. should not live a normal life out in the world. But unfortunately I cannot prove it.' ''*

Milena did not resign herself to her life in Veleslavin. She looked for a means of escape and found one. Touched by her pleas, one of the nurses supplied her with a key to the garden gate, and from then on Milena slipped out to meet Ernst Polak as often as she pleased.

At the end of nine months Jan Jesensky realized the absurdity of what he had done. Milena was released. She married Ernst Polak. Her father withdrew his financial support and broke off all relations with his daughter.

*Max Brod, *Franz Kafka, eine Biographie*, 3rd ed. (Frankfurt: S. Fischer Verlag, 1954), p. 276.

6

THE LOWEST DEPTHS

. . . I, I, Milena, know in every fiber of my being that you will be right whatever you do. . . . What would I do with you if I didn't know that? Just as in the deep sea, every tiniest spot is under the heaviest pressure, so is it with you, but any other life would be shameful. . . .

—KAFKA, *BRIEFE AN MILENA*

In 1918 Milena went to Vienna with Ernst Polak. It must have been hard for her to leave Prague, for she loved this city with its narrow streets and idyllic squares, its cafés and the little restaurants of the Old Town. . . . Milena needed the atmosphere of Prague, and she was attached to the countryside of Bohemia, her native land.

At first they lived in a run-down furnished room on Nussdorfer Strasse. Later they moved to a gloomy apartment on Lerchenfelderstrasse. Milena never really got used to Vienna; she was lonely. Her married life was beset by crises. To what extent Milena was responsible for the tension I do not know. She had character traits that are hardly conducive to a harmonious marriage. She had a sharp tongue and was capable of cruel sarcasm; but Polak was arrogant and inconsiderate, conceited and domineering. But the real reason for the breakdown of their marriage was that, like so many of the young artists and writers of the day, Polak was a believer in free love. Even before leaving Prague, he had had affairs with other women. Milena thought it her duty to be broad-minded. She tried to make herself believe that he was entitled to his freedom and affected to be "above all that," but this was only a mask behind which she hid her despair. She was young, passionate, and in love with Polak. Little by little she lost her self-assurance. Fearing that he had ceased to love her, she became frantically jealous and went to unreasonable lengths in the hope of winning back the love for which she had sacrificed so much.

Ernst Polak, who was working toward a doctorate, was an enthusiastic participant in a philosophical seminar presided over by the logical positivists Moritz Schlick and Otto Neurath, which was to become the nucleus of the "Vienna Circle." The enthusiasm of its members bordered on religious fanaticism. When the writer Felix Weltsch, an old friend from Prague, ran into Polak in Vienna, Polak told him about his studies and the thesis he was working on. Amazed at the tone in which Polak spoke of the seminar, Weltsch cried out, "But, good Lord, you people sound like a cult." To which Polak promptly replied, "Yes, that's exactly what we are!"

Ernst Polak was a habitué of the Café Herrenhof, where he and his friends met almost every afternoon and stayed until late into the night, as was then customary both in Vienna and in Prague. The cafés were the center of artistic and intellectual life; writers, painters, and philosophers would sit there for hours over a cup of black coffee, gaining inspiration from the click of the billiard balls in the back room, the street sounds, and the hum of conversation around them. In addition to Franz Werfel, whom they had known in Prague, Polak's and Milena's friends included Franz Blei, Gina and Otto Kaus, the psychoanalyst Dr. Otto Gross, Friedrich Eckstein, Hermann Broch, and Willy Haas.

Unwilling to break off their absorbing conversations, the Vienna café dwellers were in the habit of seeing one another home.

As the streetcars had long stopped running at that late hour, this custom often took them from end to end of the city, and it was sometimes broad daylight before the last good-byes were said. Once, while Milena, Werfel, and Eckstein were walking back and forth, taking one another home, a heavy rain set in. They had just arrived at Werfel's place and he suggested, first jokingly, then not so jokingly, that Milena should spend the night with him. When he took her by the arm and tried to drag her into the house, Eckstein, who had been standing in the doorway pretending not to notice, became thoroughly alarmed. To his relief the incident ended in good-natured laughter, and they all really went home.

Strangely enough, Milena didn't think much of Werfel as a writer. While still in Prague, she had been impressed by his first three books of poems, *Der Weltfreund, Wir sind*, and *Einander (Friend of All the World, We Are*, and *One Another)*, but later, comparing his work with that of others who were less successful, she came to regard his meteoric rise as unjustified. And she found Werfel's Catholicism, grafted onto his Jewish origins, rather ridiculous. But another reason for her poor opinion of Werfel may have been her increasingly strained relations with Ernst Polak, who was a close friend of Werfel's. In one of his letters to Milena, Kafka reproached her for her unfairness to Werfel. "Where is your understanding of human nature, Milena? I've doubted it on several occasions, for instance, when you wrote about Werfel, maybe there was love in what you said, and perhaps only love, nevertheless it's wrong to ignore everything else about Werfel and harp only on his fatness (and incidentally, he doesn't seem at all fat to me); in my opinion Werfel is growing more handsome and more charming from year to year, though it's true that I don't see much of him—didn't you know that only fat people are trustworthy?"*

*Kafka, *Briefe an Milena*, pp. 44–45.

Polak often brought his café friends home with him in the middle of the night. Milena, who was usually asleep by then, had to get up and sit sleepily in her dressing gown, listening to discussions of the most esoteric philosophical problems. Some of the guests would stay on for the night, and one had the strange habit of rolling up in the carpet. It was a different kind of bohemianism from what she had been used to in Prague. If she was isolated in Vienna, it may have been only because, being unhappy, she always seemed sad and distraught. Once when she joined the others at the Café Herrenhof, Franz Blei said maliciously, "Take a look at Milena; there she is again, looking like six volumes of Dostoevsky."

Milena had none of the easy charm and coquetry characteristic of Viennese women. Her beauty was of a kind that did not encourage familiarity. Her figure suggested an Egyptian statue. There was nothing soft and round about it, and she was always rather pale. One was struck by her penetrating blue eyes, which owed their special quality not to the contrast with her dark brows and lashes but to her inner fire. Her sensual lips contrasted with her firm, energetic chin. She struck people as independent and self-assured; nothing in her appearance suggested that she was in need of being protected and cosseted—yet that was just what she longed for.

Willy Haas paints the following portrait of Milena at that time: If any friend expressed a wish in her presence, and if she felt that this wish meant a great deal to him, she didn't hesitate for one moment—she took immediate action. Once Willy Haas was in urgent need of a room; he had just fallen in love. Milena arranged for the loan of a good friend's room and decorated it with armloads of flowers and shrubs. As a rule, she had hardly enough money for food, so she must have borrowed the large amount she spent on these flowers. Such generosity came naturally to Milena, and she expected the same of her friends, who only too often disappointed her.

When Willy Haas came home from the First World War, he had eight hundred crowns' worth of pay vouchers, which to his surprise he was able to redeem. On hearing that the war was over, most soldiers thought these vouchers were worthless and threw them away. But Haas, to be on the safe side, kept his. On his return, he went to see Milena and informed her of his good fortune. She was in urgent need of money and asked him to give her half. When he hesitated, she simply took the money away from him. For a few moments he was furious, but then he was ashamed. How could he have been so petty, how could he have hesitated for a second to do Milena a favor? He felt humiliated. Milena had taught him a lesson.

In his afterword to Kafka's *Letters to Milena*, Haas wrote: "She sometimes gave the impression of a noblewoman of the sixteenth or seventeenth century, a character such as Stendhal found in the old Italian chronicles and put into his novels, the Duchess of Sanseverina or Mathilde de la Mole, for example: passionate, bold, cold, and intelligent in her decisions, but reckless in her choice of means when her passion was involved—and in her younger days this was almost always the case. As a friend, she was inexhaustible, inexhaustible in kindness, inexhaustible in resources, the source of which often remained a mystery, but also inexhaustible in the demands she made on her friends, demands which she as well as her friends took for granted. . . . Out of place amid the erotic and intellectual promiscuity of Viennese café society during the wild years after 1918, she was very unhappy."*

In those difficult years in Vienna, she was determined to make her own living. It was hard because she was untrained and had no profession. She gave Czech lessons, mostly to industrialists whose factories and property after the breakup of the Austrian

*Kafka, *Briefe an Milena*, p. 274.

52

Empire were situated in Czechoslovakia. One of these was the writer Hermann Broch. At first these lessons were her only source of income. Occasionally, when she was especially short of funds and Ernst Polak gave her no money for the household, she would go to one of the railroad stations and offer her services as a porter. She was willing to do work of any kind; if she suffered, it was from heartache. Her father had rejected her, and hardly a day passed without Ernst Polak humiliating her. Deeply wounded, she withdrew into herself. She felt the ground cut from under her feet. When Kafka wrote to her later: "You who really live your life down to such depths . . ." the depths are to be taken literally.

Milena was convinced that Polak had ceased to desire her because she was poorly dressed, unable to compete with his fashionable admirers. But how was she to buy good clothes when she couldn't even afford to eat properly? A girlfriend with well-to-do parents learned of her trouble and thought up a dangerous way of helping her. She stole a valuable piece of jewelry from her parents, sold it, and gave Milena the proceeds. Milena used most of the money to pay the debts which Polak had shamelessly run up entertaining other women and which even more shamelessly he had asked Milena to pay. The rest she spent on herself. She was obsessed with this one idea: Now she would be able to put Polak to the test, now she would find out whether he really didn't love her anymore or whether he had merely grown tired of her because she was always wearing the same old dress. She went from shop to shop, putting together an outfit such as she had not known for years: the finest shoes, the most stylish dress, the most intriguing hat. Thus attired, she ran to the Café Herrenhof; with beating heart she approached the table where Ernst Polak was sitting with friends of both sexes, as he did every day. Everything depended on his reaction. Would he notice her, or as usual overlook her? When she stepped up to the table, Polak looked around, gaped at her, and said admiringly, "Why,

Milena, how chic you are today!" She responded with a resounding slap in the face. "You'll be surprised," she said, "when you find out where it all comes from."

It was only with great difficulty that the theft could be hushed up, and Milena was held responsible, as her friend had stolen for her. After that she was despised as well as isolated. There was no one who understood her, on whose shoulder she could weep. In her distress she resorted to drugs. One of her husband's friends, the one who rolled up in the carpet to sleep, gave her cocaine.

The man's name was Stein. On a visit to Prague, he went to see Kafka, who speaks of him in one of his letters to Milena. "I saw Stein again yesterday. He is one of those men toward whom everyone is unjust. I don't know why people laugh at him. He knows everybody, knows all the intimate details, and yet he is modest, his judgments are careful, intelligently nuanced, respectful; true, they are a little too obvious, too naively vain, but that only adds to his worth if one has had the experience of secret, criminal, lustful vanity. I started talking about Haas, tiptoed past Jarmila; after a while I came to your husband, and finally I got around to you—by the way, it's not true that I enjoy hearing you talked about, not at all, I just like to hear your name over and over again, all day long. If I had asked him, he would have told me about you, but as I didn't ask him he contented himself with observing that to his sincere regret you are barely alive these days, that you've been destroyed by cocaine (how thankful I was at the moment to hear that you're still alive). And incidentally, cautious and modest as he is, he added that he hadn't seen that with his own eyes but only heard about it."*

It was not easy for a woman who lived as passionately as Milena did, who, as she herself said, was "a bundle of emo-

*Kafka, *Briefe an Milena*, p. 193.

tions," to curb her wild impulses and discipline herself. That she nevertheless succeeded bears witness to her strength of character. She threw herself into a line of work to which she was suited, translation from the Czech, and wrote her first articles. At first, no doubt, this was just one more attempt to relieve her financial straits. But then she became absorbed in her new work and thus, through creative effort, regained her balance. She sent her little articles to her friend Staša in Prague, who in the meantime had become a contributor to the newspaper *Tribuna*. Milena waited with trepidation for the reply, as her first journalistic efforts struck her as incompetent and atrociously sentimental. However, they were accepted. She was proud to see herself in print and overjoyed at being able to contribute to the household expenses, though Polak took her contribution for granted. Once, in the midst of a quarrel, she made a big mistake. To impress her husband, she spoke of her journalistic success and showed him her articles. Polak read them and burst into loud laughter. She was wounded to the quick.

7

FRANZ KAFKA AND MILENA

*Either the world is so tiny or we are so enormous; in either case we fill
it completely. . . .*

—KAFKA, BRIEFE AN MILENA

Even before Milena began to talk about her relationship with
Franz Kafka, she told me one evening, as we were walking back
and forth between the barracks in the pale evening light, the
story of the commercial traveler Gregor Samsa in Kafka's *Metamorphosis*. As I was later to discover, what she told me then
was her own private version of Kafka's novella. *She* was the
commercial traveler, the helpless, misunderstood Samsa, meta-
morphosed into an enormous beetle and hidden by his family
because they were ashamed of him. She went into special detail
about the beetle's illness and how, afflicted with a wound in his
back, in which dirt and mites have become encrusted, he is left
alone to die.

In 1920 in Vienna, Milena read Kafka's first stories. Even
then she recognized his greatness, and she would look upon his
work with profound veneration as long as she lived. Kafka's
prose, she thought, was perfection itself. During her Vienna
years, her own unhappiness gave her a special feeling for his
works, and that, no doubt, is what made her decide to translate

them, though her knowledge of German was still less than perfect. She became the first translator into Czech of *The Stoker, The Judgment, Metamorphosis,* and *Contemplation.*

She sent one of her translations to his publisher and received a personal answer from the author. In the first of Kafka's letters to Milena to have been preserved,* he suggests that he may have offended her with his "notes"; apparently, he had criticized her translation, and his criticism seems to have moved Milena to go and see him. They had known each other before the decisive meeting, for they frequented the same literary circles in Prague. This may be inferred from one of the early letters, in which he writes: "It occurs to me that I can't remember any particular of your appearance, only the way you walked between the little tables as you left the café, your figure, your dress, those I can still see."†

Kafka, whose doctors had diagnosed tuberculosis, was then taking a cure in Merano. Milena went to see him there. She wrote about this meeting in her little book *The Way to Simplicity,* which appeared in 1926, though without mentioning Kafka by name. In the chapter entitled "The Curse of Sterling Qualities," she ventures the opinion that rigorously virtuous people are not necessarily the kindest, but often on the contrary are dangerous and evil, whereas men with so-called faults are not infrequently far kinder and more tolerant. She counts her own father among the "virtuous men," and curiously enough speaks of herself as his "son." "My father never told a lie in all his life, and that is quite an accomplishment. But though his son was deceitful now and then, he should not have been written off as a liar. My father, on the other hand, full of pride over his love of truth and drunk with self-esteem, is so merciless that from a pedagogical point of view it would have been better if he had been

*Kafka, *Briefe an Milena,* p. 9.
†Ibid.

obliged to tell a lie once in his life. Then he wouldn't have treated his son so cruelly."*

In her article Milena contrasts the man of "sterling qualities" with a truly good man, and that, to her way of thinking, was Franz Kafka. "I believe," she wrote, "that the best man I have ever known is a foreigner, whom I met several times in company." It soon becomes clear that this "foreigner" was Kafka, who was both a German and a Jew, for at the end of her little book she tells a story which Kafka himself had written her in a letter. "No one knew much about him, and people did not think him extraordinary. Once he was accused of some misdeed and he did not defend himself. But because he had such an honest and manly face and the accusation was a serious one, I could not believe it. It made me miserable to think that this man with the honest face and quiet eyes that looked one full in the face might have done anything despicable. So I made a point of finding out what had actually happened. His reason for not defending himself was that to do so he would have had to reveal something extremely fine and noble that he had done, something anyone else would have boasted of. I had never seen such a thing. Later I realized that he is in every way the most remarkable person I have ever known, and nothing has ever moved me as deeply as that little glimpse into his heart. He was infinitely noble, but he made a secret of it, as if he were ashamed of being in any way superior to others. He was incapable of doing anything that would have shown what he was really like, and the finest things he did were done diffidently, quietly, in secret, yes, really in secret, and not in such a way as to let everyone know he had done them in secret. When he died—I have no hesitation about saying that he was too good for this world, the phrase is justified in his case—I read in one of his diaries about an incident in his childhood. As I thought it the most beautiful

*Milena Jesenská, *The Way to Simplicity*.

58

thing I had ever read, I shall tell the story here: When he was little, his mother gave him a shilling. He was very poor, he had never had so much money, it was a big thing for him. He had earned the money and that made it even more of a big thing. He went out in the street to buy something with his money, and there he saw a beggar woman, who looked so appallingly poor that he wanted nothing more in the world than to give her his shilling. But that was in the days when a shilling was a small fortune to a beggar woman or a small boy. He so dreaded the praise and gratitude the beggar woman would lavish on him and the attention he would attract that he went away and changed the shilling. When he came back he gave the beggar woman a penny, ran around the block and, coming from the opposite direction, gave her a second penny. This he did twelve times and scrupulously gave her all twelve pennies, keeping none for himself. Then he burst into tears.

"I think this is the most beautiful fairy tale I have ever heard, and when I read it, I made up my mind that I would never forget it as long as I lived."*

The love affair between Kafka and Milena began in Merano in 1920. It was a passionate, tragic love, as can be seen from Kafka's surviving letters to Milena. When I read them, I was overwhelmed by memories of her. Everything Kafka said about her is unique in its truth. As the great writer saw her, so she was: the "loving one." To her, love was the one thing that really counted in life. She felt deeply and intensely and was not ashamed of it. To her love was something clear and self-evident. She never resorted to feminine artifice and was incapable of coquetry. She had the rare gift of sensing the loved one's feelings and she was often able to give him a full account of an emotional crisis he had gone through days before. "You know nothing about a person," she once said to me, "until you've loved him."

*Milena Jesenská, *The Way to Simplicity.*

The few of Milena's written statements about Franz Kafka to have come down to us bear witness to her profound understanding both of his genius and of his tragic illness.

Milena was twenty-four when they met; though life had treated her cruelly and she had matured beyond her years, she was young and healthy and, as she wrote later on, "very close to the earth." She loved Franz Kafka, she was in love with his "honest, manly face," his "quiet eyes that look you full in the face," and in 1920, when Wilma Lövenbach came to see her in Vienna, she said to her friend, "Do you know Franz Kafka? A wonderful man."

She overwhelmed him with letters and telegrams, and the more he hesitated the more urgently she insisted on his coming to see her. They had four happy days together in Vienna. "The chestnut trees were in bloom," she told me. But even at that meeting the first shadows seem to have fallen on their love. As she wrote much later in a letter to Max Brod, if she had been a "mere female," their days in Vienna would probably have meant the end of their love.

But the bond between Kafka and the young, strong Milena with her "life-giving power" was far more than physical. "Your most beautiful letters," he wrote to her, "and that means a good deal, for all of them, almost every line of them, are the most beautiful thing that has ever come my way, are those in which you concur with my 'fear' and at the same time try to explain why there's no need for me to be afraid. For I too, though I may sometimes look like the suborned advocate of my 'fear,' probably concur with it deep down; indeed, it is my substance and probably the best part of me. And since it is the best part of me, perhaps that alone is what you love. For what else is so lovable about me? But this is lovable.

"And once when you asked how with fear in my heart I could call that Saturday 'good,' it is easily explained. Since I love you (*and I do love you, you dull-witted thing, as the sea loves a tiny pebble on the bottom, my love inundates you in exactly the same way*, and I'll be a pebble with you, if heaven permits), I love the whole world, which includes your left shoulder, no, it was the right one first, so I kiss it if I choose (and if you'll be kind enough to pull your blouse down), and this includes your left shoulder too, and your face above me in the woods and your face below me in the woods, and me resting on your almost bare bosom. So you're right when you say that we were already one, and of that I have no fear at all; on the contrary, it's all my pride and joy, and I don't restrict it to the woods.

"But the fact is that between this day-world and the 'half hour in bed' that you once spoke of contemptuously as 'men's business' there's an abyss that I can't bridge, probably because I don't want to. The other side is an affair of the night, utterly and in every sense an affair of the night; on this side lies the world I possess, and now you want me to jump across, to leap into the night and take possession of it again. Can one take possession of anything *again*? Wouldn't that be to lose it? Here is the world that I possess, and you want me to cross over for the sake of some sinister magic, some hocus-pocus, some philosophers' stone, some alchemy, some wishing ring. No, no, no, I'm terribly afraid of it.

"To try and catch in one night by magic, hastily, breathing heavily, helpless, possessed, to catch by magic what every day offers to my open eyes! ('Maybe' children can't be had in any other way; 'maybe' children, too, are magic. Let's leave the question open for now.) That's why I'm so grateful to you (to you and everything else) and that's why it is *samozřejmé* [self-evident] that by your side I am supremely quiet and supremely unquiet, supremely constrained and supremely free, and why, having understood this, I've given up all other life. Look into my eyes."*

*Kafka, *Briefe an Milena*, pp. 148 ff.

61

Milena suffered all her life from guilt feelings and despised herself for every failure. Her breach with her father was a great blow to her and she never fully got over it. At the time of her love for Kafka, the wound was still open. Who could have understood her feelings better than Kafka, whose conflict with his own father tormented him as long as he lived? But their relationships with their fathers were very different. Milena's was emotional and therefore stronger and more painful than Kafka's. He never fully understood Milena's feelings in the matter. On one occasion he wrote: "I understand your despair over your father's letter only insofar as every new reminder of this painful relationship, which has already lasted so long, is bound to renew your despair. After all, you can't read anything new into his letter. Even I, who have never had a letter from your father, find nothing new in it. It is affectionate and tyrannical, he thinks he has to be tyrannical if he is to be affectionate. The signature means very little, it is only the emblem of the tyrant; above it, after all, he has written '*lito*' [sorry] and '*strašne smutně*' [terribly sorry], and that makes up for everything.

"Possibly, on the other hand, you are horrified by the disproportion between your letter and his; well, I haven't seen your letter, but you should consider the disproportion between his 'obvious willingness' and your 'incomprehensible' obstinacy.

"Are you in doubt about your answer? Or rather, were you in doubt? For you write that now you would know what to write. That is strange. If you had already answered and were to ask me, 'What did I write?' I would tell you without hesitation what I thought you had written.

"Of course there can be no doubt that in your father's mind there is no difference between your husband and me; in the eyes of a European we both have the same negroid features, but apart from the fact that you can't say anything definite about it for the moment, why should you mention it in your answer? And why should a lie be necessary?

"I think you can only answer what someone who, observing your life intently and with beating heart and seeing hardly anything else, would have to say to your father if he had spoken of you as he has: 'All propositions,' all 'set conditions' are absurd, Milena is living her own life and will not be able to live any other. Milena's life may be sad, but it is undoubtedly as 'healthy and calm' as in a sanatorium. Milena merely implores you to accept this fact; otherwise she asks you for nothing, and least of all for an 'arrangement.' She merely asks you not to be stubborn, not to shut her out, but to do as your heart bids you and speak to her as equal to equal. Once you do that, you will have relieved Milena's life of much of its sadness, and you won't have to feel 'sorry' for her anymore."*

Milena was full of contradictions. She had a woman's tenderness and a man's determination. She was at once modest, chaste, and forward. She must soon have realized that her love for Kafka had no future. But it's hard for a lover to give up hope. In one of his letters, Kafka wrote: "You mustn't say that two hours of life are unquestionably better than two pages of writing. . . ."† One can only infer that she said just that and meant it. And in another letter: ". . . and now Milena calls me with a voice that speaks with equal force to my reason and my heart . . . she is like the ocean, as powerful as the ocean which with its great mass of water, yet devoid of understanding, surges with all its might at the command of the dead and, what's more, distant moon. She doesn't know me, and perhaps it's because she suspects the truth that she urges me to come."‡ Kafka feared the magical influence on women of the distant moon.

He came a second time. The lovers met at Gmünd on the border between Austria and Czechoslovakia. Those were trou-

*Kafka, *Briefe an Milena*, pp. 161 ff.
†Ibid., p. 44.
‡Ibid., p. 68.

63

bled times, and it seems certain that Milena, who had become an Austrian through her marriage to Ernst Polak, was unable to obtain a Czech visa. But Gmünd was not the answer. Their love found no sexual consummation. In a letter Kafka tries to find an explanation: "I won't write about Gmünd anymore, at least not on purpose. A good deal could be said about it, but in the end it would only amount to saying that our first day in Vienna would have been no better if I had left that same evening, though Vienna had the advantage over Gmünd that I arrived there half dead with fear and exhaustion, while in Gmünd, fool that I was, I was wonderfully self-assured without knowing it, as though nothing could happen to me ever again, like someone coming home to his own house; strange that with all the anxiety that never ceases to pervade me, I should be capable of this sort of slump into possessiveness; indeed, it may be my worst fault, in this and other matters. . . ."* And much later, on January 18, 1922, he wrote in his diary: "What have I done with the gift of sex? It's been a failure, no doubt about that. But it might have been successful. M. was right. Fear is wholly to blame. . . ."†

In a letter to Max Brod that shows her profound understanding of Kafka, Milena tries to explain why he was afraid of love: She writes: "I could spend days and nights answering your letter. You ask me why Franz is afraid of love. But I think it's something different. He sees life very differently from other people. To him, for instance, money, the stock market, exchange bureaus, a typewriter are absolutely mystical things (as indeed they are, though not to our kind of people); to him they are the weirdest puzzle, and he doesn't see them as we do. Take his work at the insurance company; does he regard it as just a job? To him any job—even his own—is as mysterious, as marvelous, as a locomotive is to a small child. The simplest things

---

*Kafka, *Briefe an Milena*, p. 213.
†Franz Kafka, *Tagebücher* (Frankfurt: S. Fischer Verlag, 1951), pp. 555 ff.

in the world are beyond him. Have you ever been in a post office with him? Have you seen him composing a telegram, then shaking his head, looking for the window that strikes his fancy, running from window to window without the faintest idea why, until he finds the right one. Then he pays, counts his change, finds he's been given a crown too much, and gives it back to the girl at the window. He walks slowly away, counting his change again. On the bottom step it comes to him that the crown he has given back is really his. I'm standing there beside him and I don't know what to say. He shifts his weight from foot to foot, wondering what to do. It would be hard to go back, because by that time there's a long line at the window. 'Why not let it go?' I suggest. He gives me a horrified look. 'How can I let it go?' he says. 'Not that I care about the crown. But it wouldn't be right. There's a crown too little. How can I let it go?' He goes on and on, he's terribly annoyed with me. The same thing happens in every store, every restaurant, with every beggar woman, in every conceivable variation. Once he gave a beggar woman two crowns and asked her to give him back a crown. She said she didn't have a crown. We stood there for two minutes, wondering what to do. Finally it occurred to him that he could let her keep the two crowns. But we'd only gone a few steps when I saw that he wasn't at all pleased. The same man would be only too glad to give me twenty thousand crowns. But if I asked him for twenty thousand crowns and we had to go somewhere to change money and we didn't know where, he would ponder seriously what to do about a single crown that I didn't really have coming to me. He has almost the same anxiety about women as about money. And the same with his job. Once I wired, phoned, and wrote, imploring him in God's name to come and spend a day with me. I needed him badly just then. I begged him on bended knee. He lay awake whole nights, tormenting himself. He wrote me letters full of self-recrimina- tion, but he didn't come. Why not? Because he couldn't ask for

65

leave. He couldn't ask his department head, the one he whole-heartedly admires (in all seriousness) because he can type so fast. He simply couldn't tell him he was coming to see me. Why not tell him something else? Another horrified letter. What? Lie? Tell the department head a lie? Impossible. If you ask him why he loved his first fiancée, he says, 'She was so efficient.' And he beams with admiration.

"Yes, this whole world is and remains a puzzle to him. A mystery. Something utterly beyond him, but which with his touchingly pure naïveté he admires for its efficiency. When I told him about my husband, who's unfaithful to me a hundred times a year, but has a kind of fascination for me and a lot of other women, his face lit up with the same admiration as when he told me about his department head who was a fine man because he typed so fast or as when he spoke of his fiancée, who was so 'efficient.' Such things are strange to him. A man who types fast and a man with four mistresses baffle him as much as a crown at the post office or the crown he gave the beggar woman, they baffle him because they're a part of my life. Because Franz can't live. He is incapable of living. Franz will never get well. Franz will die soon.

"The fact is that we all seem capable of living, because at some time or other we have taken refuge in a lie, in blindness, in enthusiasm, in optimism, in some conviction, in pessimism or something of the sort. He has never taken refuge in anything. He is absolutely incapable of lying, just as he is incapable of getting drunk. He has nothing to take refuge in, no shelter. It's as if he were naked and everyone else had clothes on. And what he says, what he is and experiences, is not even the truth. His being is resolutely self-contained and self-sufficient, devoid of all artifice that might enable him to misrepresent life, either its beauty or its misery. There is nothing heroic about his asceti-cism—and that makes it all the greater and nobler. All heroism is falsehood and cowardice. This is not a man for whom asceticism is a means to an end; it is a man whose fearful clear-sightedness, purity, and inability to compromise compel him to be ascetic.

"There are other highly intelligent people who are unwilling to compromise. But as they wear magic spectacles which distort their vision, they have no need of compromise. They can type fast and have lots of women. He stands beside them and marvels at them; he marvels at everything, including typewriters and women. He will never understand.

"His books are amazing. He himself is infinitely more amazing. . . ."*

The love affair, which had long been confined to letters, finally ended at Kafka's wish. He was very sick, and Milena's vitality weighed on him. She wanted all his love, including the physical love he dreaded. The greatness as well as the hopelessness of this passion can be inferred from the two despairing letters she wrote Max Brod after Kafka put an end to the affair. The first letter runs: "Forgive me for not being able to write in German. Perhaps you know enough Czech to understand. Forgive me for bothering you. But I'm at my wits' end; my mind is a blank, I know nothing and feel nothing. It seems to me that something terrible has happened to me in these months, but I don't know much about it. I don't know anything about the world; I only feel that I would kill myself if I could somehow think about the very thing that eludes my mind.

"I could tell you how and why all this happened; I could tell you all about myself and about my life; but what for?—and besides, I don't know. All I know is this letter I have in my hand, that Franz wrote me from the Tatra. There's a deadly request in it, which is really an order: 'Don't write, make sure we don't meet, don't protest, this alone can enable me to carry

*Brod, *Franz Kafka, eine Biographie*, pp. 280 ff.

on with some sort of life, any other way would keep on destroying me.' I don't dare ask any questions or write a single word, nor do I know what I want of you. I don't know—I don't know what I want to know. Jesus Christ, I could squeeze my temples into my brain. Just tell me one thing, you have been with him recently, you must know: Am I to blame or not? I implore you for the love of God, don't try to comfort me, don't tell me that no one is to blame, don't give me any psychoanalysis. I know all that, I know everything you could write. . . .

"Please try to understand what I want. I know all about Franz; I know what has happened and I don't know what has happened; I'm on the brink of madness; I've tried to do right, to live, to think, to feel according to my conscience, but there is blame somewhere. That's what I want you to tell me. . . . I want to know if I'm to blame that Franz is suffering and has suffered because of me as he did because of the other women he has known; I want to know if that made his illness worse and drove him to escape from me into his fear, so now I have to disappear; I want to know if I'm to blame, or if it's the fault of his own nature. Am I making myself clear? I *must* know. You are the only person who may know something. I beg you to tell me the plain, unvarnished truth, even if it's brutal to tell me what you really think. . . ."*

At the end of her next letter to Max Brod she writes: " . . . every day I go to the post office. I can't get out of the habit. . . ." For two years she kept going. The general delivery window was inseparable from her love. Kafka never wrote to her at home for fear of Ernst Polak. Once during the winter of 1922 Wilma saw her hurrying down the street. Driving past in her car, she called her by name, and Milena turned her head. Her eyes were blank, her face pale and drawn, and she seemed unaware of her surroundings. In another letter to Max Brod she tries to explain

*Brod, *Franz Kafka, eine Biographie*, pp. 282 ff.

"how and why it all happened" and where she was at fault. "Thank you for your kindness," it begins. "In the meantime I have more or less come to my senses. I can think again. That doesn't make me feel any better. It goes without saying that I won't write to Franz. How could I? If it's true that we have a task to perform on this earth, I've performed mine very badly where he is concerned. How could I be so selfish as to harm him when I was unable to help him? As for his fear, I know it down to the last fiber. He had it before me, before he knew me. I knew his fear before I knew him. I armed myself against it by understanding it. In the four days he spent with me he lost it. We laughed at it. I am sure no sanatorium will succeed in curing him. He will never get well as long as he has this fear. And no psychological treatment can overcome his fear, because his fear will stand in the way of any treatment. His fear applies not only to me, but to everything that is shamelessly alive, to the flesh, for instance. The flesh is too naked, he can't bear the sight of it.

"In those days I managed to overcome that fear. When he felt it, he looked into my eyes, we waited awhile, as if we were out of breath, as if our feet hurt, and after a while it went away. No effort was needed; everything was clear and simple. I dragged him up a hill outside Vienna; he walked slowly, so I went ahead; he trudged along behind me; when I close my eyes, I can still see his white shirt and his sunburnt neck and the effort he was making. He walked all day, uphill and down; he walked in the sun, he didn't cough once, he ate like a horse and slept soundly, he was just plain healthy, and during those days his sickness was no worse than a slight cold. If I had gone to Prague with him, I would have kept the same place in his heart. But both my feet were solidly planted in the ground of Vienna, I was unable to leave my husband, and maybe I was too much of a woman to submit to what I well knew would be a life of strict asceticism. And besides, I have an uncontrollable longing, a desperate longing for a very different life from the one I am leading and will probably go on leading, for a life with a child, a life close to the earth.

"That was probably what got the better of everything, of love, of the will to fly, of admiration, and again of love. Anything more I could say about it would be a lie. But maybe that's the least of it. And anyway, by then it was too late. My inner conflict was too evident, and that frightened him. Because that was just what he'd been fighting against all his life, from the other side. With me he was able to rest. And then it began to torment him even when he was with me. Against my will. I knew perfectly well that something had happened, something that could not be undone. I was too weak to do the one and only thing that I knew would have helped him. There I was to blame. And you know I was to blame. The very thing that people put down to Franz's abnormality is what makes him superior. The women he knew before were commonplace women, capable only of a female existence. I prefer to think that all of us, the whole world and everybody in it, are sick, and that he alone is healthy, right-thinking, right-feeling, and pure. I know he doesn't fight against life but only against that kind of life. If I had succeeded in going away with him, he would have been able to live happily with me. But I didn't know all this until now. Then I was a commonplace woman like all the women in the world, a little female at the mercy of her instincts. And that was where his fear came from. He was right. For he is incapable of feeling anything that is not right. He knows ten thousand times more about the world than all the people in the world. And his fear is right. You're mistaken, Franz will not write to me of his own accord. There's nothing he could say. There's not a single word he could say to me in his fear. I know he loves me. He is too good and too upright to stop loving me. He would think it wrong. He always regards himself as the weak and guilty party. And yet no one else in the whole world has his immense strength, his unswerving

70

striving for perfection, purity, and truth. That is the truth. Down to my last drop of blood I know it. Only I can't bring myself to see it fully and clearly. When I do, it will be terrible. I race through the streets, I sit whole nights at the window. Sometimes my thoughts jump about like the little sparks when you sharpen a knife, and my heart hangs on a fishhook, you know, one of those thin little hooks, and it digs into me with terrible cutting pain. . . ."*

The regular correspondence ended at Kafka's bidding. But a few sentences that he wrote later to Max Brod tell us something about his feeling for Milena: "You will talk with Milena, I shall never again have that joy. When you talk to her about me, speak as if I were dead, I mean, where my 'outside,' my 'extraterritoriality,' is concerned. When Ehrenstein came to see me recently, he said more or less that in M. life was holding out a hand to me and I had the choice between life and death; that was a little too high-sounding, not in regard to Milena but to me, but essentially true; the only stupid part was that he seemed to believe that a choice was open to me. If there were still a Delphic oracle, I'd have consulted it, and it would have replied, 'A choice between life and death? How can you hesitate?' "†

Milena went on sending Kafka letters and postcards at long intervals, and she went to see him a few times at his parents' house in Prague. On January 19, 1922, Kafka noted in his diary: ". . . the last visits were as usual affectionate and proud, but a little tired, a little forced, like visits to a sickroom. Is this impression right? Did you find something decisive against me in the *Diaries*?"‡ To judge by an entry in Kafka's diary, she came to see him for the last time in May 1922, but it is thought that she saw him later, when he was very ill. I don't know. But I do

---

*Brod, *Franz Kafka, eine Biographie*, pp. 285 ff.
†Kafka, *Briefe an Milena*, p. 322.
‡Kafka, *Tagebücher*, pp. 553 ff.

know that she loved him to the end, as is shown by her deeply moving obituary:

"FRANZ KAFKA. The day before yesterday, Franz Kafka, a German writer living in Prague, died at the Kierling Sanatorium in Klosterneuburg near Vienna. Few people knew him here in Prague, for he was a recluse, a wise man who was afraid of life. He had been suffering for years with lung trouble, and though he was being treated for it, he also deliberately cultivated it and encouraged it psychologically. 'When the heart and soul can no longer bear the burden, the lungs take over half of it, and then the burden is more or less evenly distributed,' he once wrote in a letter, and that was the attitude he took toward his illness. It gave him a sensibility bordering on the miraculous and a terrifyingly uncompromising moral purity; conversely, he was a man who let his illness bear the whole burden of his fear of life. He was shy, timid, gentle, and good, but the books he wrote were cruel and painful. He saw a world full of invisible demons that make war on helpless human beings and destroy them. He was clear-sighted, too wise to live and too weak to fight. But this was the weakness of fine and noble beings who are incapable of fighting against fear, misunderstandings, unkindness, and untruth, who acknowledge their weakness from the start, submit, and so put the victor to shame. He understood his fellow men in a way that is possible only for those who live alone, whose perceptions are so subtly tuned that they can read a whole man in a fleeting play of the features. His knowledge of the world was vast and deep. He himself was a vast and deep world. He wrote the most important books in recent German literature. They embody in untendentious form the battle of the generations in our time. They are genuinely naked and therefore seem naturalistic even when they speak in symbols. They have the dry irony and second sight of a man who saw the world so clearly that he could not bear it and had to die, for he was unwilling to make concessions, to take refuge, as others do, in

72

intellectual delusions, however noble. Dr. Franz Kafka wrote *The Stoker* (a fragment, published in Czech in Neumann's *Cerven*), which constitutes the first chapter of a beautiful, still unpublished novel; *The Judgment*, dealing with the conflict between the generations; *Metamorphosis*, which is the most powerful book in modern German literature; *In the Penal Colony*; and the sketches *Contemplation* and *The Country Doctor*. The last novel, *The Trial*, has for years been complete in manuscript, ready for publication; it is one of those books whose impact on the reader is so overwhelming that all comment is superfluous. All his books deal with unwarranted guilt feelings and with the horror of mysterious misunderstandings. As a man and an artist he was so infinitely scrupulous that he remained alert even where others, the deaf, felt secure."*

*Milena Jesenská, "Notes of the Day," *Národní Listy*, July 6, 1924 (German translation, *Forum 9*, Vienna, p. 97).

8

THE WAY TO SIMPLICITY

In the spring of 1924 Milena's friend Wilma came to see her in Vienna. Milena was by nature reserved and seldom spoke of her private life. "One must learn to keep one's distance," she once wrote. "It is possible to see people day in, day out, without revealing one's inner self. They may in the end get a glimpse of one's private life, but there's no need to help them. Too much familiarity exposes one to criticism, pity, and envy; it opens the door to misunderstandings and at that point all human relations become problematic."

Yet despite Milena's reserve Wilma could see at a glance that she had changed; she was in better health, calmer, and more poised. She told her visitor not without pride that she had recently started a kind of *pension* in her apartment. She let two rooms and provided her roomers with a midday meal; she had even hired a maid. She really seemed to have taken hold of herself. She had learned to cook and keep house, talents which were later in Prague to benefit any number of impoverished guests.

Wilma soon learned that Milena had at last summoned up the strength to break with Ernst Polak and put an end to a marriage which had long been in ruins, and that she had found happiness in a new love.

"May I introduce my lodger, Xaver Count Schaffgotsch?" said Milena rather hesitantly, as though apologizing for the title.

A charming young man entered the room, and the somewhat stodgy Wilma observed with satisfaction that he had excellent manners. "He was a blessing," she noted, "after all the intellectual louts who ordinarily surrounded Milena. At last someone who showed her the flattering attentions that every woman deserves. . . ."

Later on, Milena assured Wilma that Xaver was not a typical aristocrat, but rather, an aristocratic outsider. Schaffgotsch was a former Austrian officer who had been in Russia at the time of the revolution and become a Communist. Through him Milena came into contact with Communist circles. In 1925 she left Vienna for good; she and Xaver went to stay with Alice Gerstl, an old friend of hers from Prague, and her husband Otto Rühle, at Buchholtz-Friedenwald near Dresden. The Rühles lived in an attractive house on a hill not far from the White Stag in Hellerau.

Rühle was more than twenty years older than his wife. Before the First World War he had belonged to the left wing of the German Social Democratic party and been a member of the Reichstag. In 1914, along with Karl Liebknecht, he had voted against the war credits. In 1916 he had helped to organize the Spartacus League and in 1918 had been a founder of the Communist party. But as an antiauthoritarian leftist, he found himself in opposition to the party only a year later and left it, never to return. Rühle and his fellow oppositionists already realized that "in the event of a victorious revolution the dictatorship of the proletariat would be replaced by a dictatorship of the party and its leadership." Yet Rühle remained a Marxist as long as he lived. His last book, *Living Thoughts of Marxism*, was written in collaboration with Leon Trotsky in Mexico, where they were both living in exile. A teacher by profession, Rühle also published numerous works on education, seen from a Marxist standpoint, including *The Proletarian Child*, *Association with Children*, and *The Neglected Child*.

And in collaboration with his wife, Alice, who was a disciple of the psychoanalyst Alfred Adler, Rühle wrote a number of articles and a book on modern psychology.

In 1925, when Milena and Xaver came to Buchholtz, Rühle was the owner of Am andern Ufer (On the Other Bank), a publishing house in Dresden which had published several of his works. Alice, a cultivated woman of Milena's generation, well versed in music, art, and literature, set the tone in the Rühle household. She guided her guests around Dresden, introducing them to its beautiful baroque buildings, and taking them to the theater and art shows. Milena, who was very close to Alice, felt at home in her house. She and Schaffgotsch stayed there for almost ten months.

At that time, in addition to her journalism, Milena was working on a Czech edition of *Peter Pan*, to be published at Christmas 1925 by the Akciová tiskárna Children's Library. A young acquaintance of hers in Prague, Jirka Malá, was doing the translation. When she finished, Milena invited her to Buchholtz to discuss it. Jirka arrived full of eager anticipation and was met at the station by Milena and Schaffgotsch. She was a well-bred young lady, and from the start she was thoroughly bewildered by the behavior of her hosts. The aristocratic young man grabbed her bag, tossed it on a hand truck, and moved off like a professional porter. As she later confided, she felt that he was "overdoing the hospitality" and that his conduct was "too too proletarian." She kept her thoughts to herself but was unable to conceal her embarrassment. Milena saved the situation by explaining that she and Xaver were expert porters, having learned the trade at the Franz Josef Station in Vienna. And she added, "Xaver is even more experienced than I am; during the famine in Russia, he even used to unload sacks from ships in Odessa."

The unsuspecting Jirka was to have further grounds for amazement at Milena's new surroundings and the change that had come over her. Marxist debates were the order of the day in the Rühle household, and Milena, who up until then had been quite unpolitical, not only seemed to enjoy them but revealed a knowledge of matters which to the young visitor were a complete mystery. She sat silent, feeling hopelessly inferior and convinced that Milena must be dreadfully disappointed by her ignorance.

To her relief, the subject was changed and they started going over her translation together. Now she was on firm ground. She was enormously impressed by Milena's feeling for language. Though she knew no English, she had a remarkable gift for finding the mot juste in Czech. Stimulated by their work, the three women recalled beloved Czech poems and took turns in reciting. Schaffgotsch joined in with an ample repertory of German poetry. On this occasion, the visitor learned that Schaffgotsch not only wrote fairy tales but was working on a play that was later published by Malik Verlag. Jirka noted with relief that they had other interests beside Marxism and communism. For her, the high point of the evening was still to come. They played music together. Jirka played the fiddle, while Alice and Milena took turns in accompanying her at the piano. In the ensuing discussion Schaffgotsch proved to be something of a musicologist.

Milena had contributed for years to the Czech daily *Tribuna*, making a name for herself as the Vienna fashion correspondent. Then, shortly before she and Xaver Schaffgotsch left for Dresden, she was temporarily reconciled with her father, and he recommended her to his party newspaper, the national conservative *Národní Listy*. Her father and Aunt Ružena were both filled with pride at the general recognition of Milena's journalistic talents, and her promotion to the *Národní Listy* was to her a real triumph. She owed her success, not to her father's influence, but to her own ability and hard work, though she herself did not think much of herself as a writer. "The only thing I can really write," she judged, "is love letters, and when you come right down to it, my articles are just that."

Over the years she developed both as a human being and as a writer. The direction of her development is suggested by the title she gave to a collection of her articles which appeared in 1926: *The Way to Simplicity*. The book was a sort of letter to her father, and indeed she dedicated it "To my dear Father," with whom she longed to be permanently reconciled. She brought it to him with the plea that he should try to understand her in spite of everything, and that he would not, like Kafka's father, leave it unread "on his bedside table."

Milena's return to Prague in 1925 was an unexpected triumph. When she left in 1918, she had been under a cloud. "Good" Czech society had found it hard to swallow her friendship with Staša, the Veleslavín incident, her way of dressing, sometimes in flowing robes and sometimes in rumpled skirt and blouse, and to top it all, her marriage to a "German Jew." The Milena who returned was a different woman. In the flower of her beauty, a well-known reporter, courted by dressmakers, herself smartly dressed, though with the simplicity that was her hallmark, and above all, on the staff of the *Národní Listy*, the leading national-conservative newspaper of Prague. Invitations poured in from all sides. But Milena declined most of them; she preferred the company of the artists and intellectuals she had frequented before going away. With them, with members of the Czech, German, and Jewish intelligentsia, she spent happy hours at the Metro Café, the Národní Kavárna, the Slavia, and occasionally the Unionka. She enjoyed her work and was glad to be alive. Her exuberance becomes understandable when we consider that she had come from run-down, impoverished Vienna to a city striving with youthful vitality to make up for three hundred years as a neglected provincial backwater. The Prague art world was bustling with life. This was the time of the first jazz, which Milena, an enthusiastic dancer, loved dearly. Friends met in cafés during the day, in the evening at bars or private parties. Compared with Vienna, Prague was a small town, everyone knew everyone else. Milena had many friends, though she also had her enemies.

It was her fate to be adored or hated; no one was indifferent to her. While some admirers went so far as to liken her to Atjka, the heroine of Romain Rolland's novel *L'Ame enchantée*, others spread malicious gossip about her past.

Even after the hard years in Vienna, during which she had learned to work regularly and submit to discipline, Milena was not exactly a well-balanced character. With her ideas about honor and chivalry she was a kind of feminine Don Quixote. She made high moral demands on herself and others and was unwilling to compromise. Living in constant conflict, she was vulnerable and often impatient. With her violent temper, her sharp tongue, and her ever-readiness to step in where she suspected an injustice, she was bound to make enemies.

The Czech Communist poet Nezval, who disliked Milena as much as she disliked him, once when he had had too much to drink at a party became obstreperous and was thrown out. He lay in the street, and no one lifted a finger to help him until Milena appeared. Indignant, she defended him against the passersby who had gathered around. She stayed with him until an ambulance arrived. Such behavior came naturally to Milena. It had nothing to do with likes or dislikes.

Milena edited the woman's page of the *Národní Listy* and also wrote about interior decoration and fashions. The Topič publishing house brought out a pamphlet of hers entitled *People Make Clothes*. Her articles on fashions were most unusual. Kafka made fun of them in one of his letters. "In reading [such an article]," he wrote, "I feel like a giant who holds out his arms to protect you from the public (he has a hard time of it, because he wants to keep the public away but at the same time not to

79

miss a word or to lose sight of you for a second), that probably demented, abysmally stupid, and to make matters worse, feminine public, who are probably shouting, 'Where is fashion? Will fashion ever get here? So far we haven't seen anything but Milena.' "*

On her return to Prague, Milena had rented a comfortable furnished room on Grosspriorplatz in the Malá Strama. She loved the Malá Strama, for it recalled many memories, especially of her grandmother whom she had been very fond of as a child. She describes her in "Maminká," one of her last articles: "My grandmother looked exactly like Božena Němcova's *Babička*. . . . She wore a silk headscarf and raised azaleas on her window ledge. She had eight children. When she baked yeast cakes, she could never make enough of them, because the children ate them straight out of the pan. . . . It took her almost half a day to knead and roll the dough for dumplings. If one of the children came down with a contagious disease, the other seven would be sure to catch it. And Grandmother, a small woman, anxious and loving, would go tripping from one little bed to another. But she herself never got sick; she had no time for it. The circle of light on the table under the lampshade, admirable economy of words coupled with admirable kindness, immense vitality and deep-rooted love of her country—all that was my grandmother. During the First World War, when 'summer time' was introduced and the day began an hour earlier, my grandmother despised it as an 'Austrian invention.' In defiance of all regulations, her clocks continued to observe reliable old sun time. When the clock in the steeple struck twelve, she, ordinarily so soft-spoken, raised her voice to announce in the tone of a queen making a solemn proclamation: 'It is now eleven o'clock'; and in her house it *was* eleven o'clock."

-----

*Kafka, *Briefe an Milena*, p. 142.

Milena had been abroad for seven years. In that time Prague had expanded considerably; the once leisurely provincial town had become a bustling metropolis. The streets swarmed with people, and not only on weekdays; on Sunday, organized groups would leave town for the mountains and other excursion sites. Frightened and horrified, Milena watched the crowds pouring into the stations on Sunday mornings. "There is something crushing about these crowds. They are too big, too massive.

"I love life, magical life in all its manifestations, all its forms, everyday life and holiday life, its surface as well as its depths. . . ."*

One day in Ravensbrück Milena talked to me about a work by the Czech writer Karel Čapek, *The War with the Newts*, a gruesome fable about an ancient mariner who somewhere in the Pacific discovers a colony of highly intelligent newts (or salamanders), who show an astonishing resemblance to humans. Realizing that they can perform simple human tasks, international capitalists round them up and exploit their labor power. But the salamanders become more and more interested in the sophisticated technology of the human workers and in an astonishingly short time acquire a high degree of technical proficiency. The explanation lies in the underdeveloped brain of the salamanders. Since they have no thoughts to distract them from work, they learn in no time to imitate human civilization. As they reproduce more quickly than human beings, they soon run short of living space. They declare war on mankind.

A primitive young Russian woman who worked at the Ravensbrück button-sewing machine in the SS tailor shop had a phenomenal ability to make her two hands do two different things at the same time. She was able to exceed the norm set by the SS by a hundred percent. "Good Lord," cried Milena,

*Milena Jesenská, "People in Movement," *Přítomnost*, April 12, 1924.

"that must be one of Čapek's salamanders. God help us if they send us millions of them."

In Buchholtz, where Milena and Schaffgotsch stayed for almost a year, they had lived as on an island. They belonged to the inner circle of the Rühle family, and Milena's friends adopted Schaffgotsch as a matter of course. Milena and Xaver had the same interests and Schaffgotsch helped her with her journalism. Together, they lived a full and happy life.

When they came to Prague together, all this changed. To Milena, Prague was home, a place where she had her habits and friends; to Schaffgotsch it was a strange city, where he knew no one. He had neither the energy nor the ability to make his way in this strange environment. He became totally dependent on Milena and followed her about like a shadow. As he kept turning up in cafés, always looking for Milena, he came to be nicknamed "Where's Milena?"

Milena tried through her connections to find him work, but in vain. The more she tried to help him, the more he blamed her for his failure. They began to get on each other's nerves and Schaffgotsch turned away from her. Once in Ravensbrück, when we were talking about men, Milena said: "I seem to have been fated to love weak men. None of them really took care of me and protected me. It's not good for a woman to be too independent. Men don't like it for very long, and that even goes for weak men. After a while, they find themselves another woman, a delicate little thing, who sits on the sofa with her hands in her lap and looks up at them admiringly. Most of my successors were like that. And many's the time I saw my impractical, helpless, oh so intellectual man miraculously transformed. I'd see him running upstairs and down for his new woman, finding apartments, going to the tax office, applying for passports, and so on. Some of them even started making money."

82

9

MARRIAGE AND ILLNESS

It's only natural that you refuse to be pitied because of this alleged law
[that everything has to be paid for].
  As for me, I believe in your law, but I do not believe that it governs
your life so cruelly, exclusively and definitively; true, it's an experience
you've had along the way, but the way is endless. . . .

—KAFKA, *BRIEFE AN MILENA*

In the summer of 1926, the younger members of Mánes, the
Creative Artists' Association, went on an excursion to Zbraslav.
Milena was invited. The rallying point was the new Mánes building, a cultural center with exhibition rooms, a restaurant, and
a café with a large terrace overlooking the river.

That summer day the party embarked on the *Primator Dit-*
trich, an asthmatic little excursion steamer. Slowly the city disappeared from sight until nothing could be seen of it but the
huge silhouette of the Hradčany and on the opposite bank the
green, bushy Petřín Hill. The air was balmy, the water as smooth
as glass. On one side, the legendary Vyšehrad, with its memories
of Princess Libuša, glided past on its rocky hill. Then the banks
leveled out, and the new housing developments of the expanding
city alternated with ugly industrial sites. Soon both banks became more countrified. The little hilltop church of Zlichov hove

into sight and a cleft in the chain of hills opened up a view deep into the back country.

The steamer chugged past the old inn at Chuchle, a popular excursion site. Milena gives a loving description of one such garden restaurant in the days before the First World War. "There are bushy chestnut trees in the garden; Japanese lanterns rock in the wind, the band of some infantry regiment is playing and the thud of bowling balls is heard in the distance. . . . Workmen are sitting at wooden tables with their wives and daughters. Young salesmen arrive in patent-leather shoes and heavily padded shoulders to dance on the covered wooden floor in the garden. It's almost unbelievable how well they dance, with what concentration and devotion; they hold their fingers stiffly at the proper distance from their partner's waist, so as not to soil her dress with their sweaty hands. Mark after mark is made on the beer mats under the glasses, until the sun sets behind the chestnut trees, the lanterns are lighted and the stars appear over the treetops. . . ."*

The river grew wider, and rich meadows spread out on both sides as far as the mouth of the Berounka, a tributary of the Vltava, bordered by willows and alders and twining its way through a chain of wooded hills.

The excursionists make merry and dance to the music of a raucous gramophone. At length the great baroque façade of Zbraslav castle comes into view. The steamer pulls up at the dock, where the excursionists are welcomed by Dr. Vančura, the local doctor, who was executed by the National Socialists some years later. Instead of visiting the castle and the town, the excursionists take the primitive ferry to the hospitable Závist tavern with its lovely garden shaded by linden trees. Here most of the party settle down to beer and sandwiches. But a small group, Milena among them, goes exploring. A path leads up-

*Milena Jesenská, "People in Movement."

ward through dense foliage to a large, shady park. Peering through the low branches of a big copper beech, the explorers discover the long, graceful, beautifully proportioned pink façade of the Archbishop's Palace, an edifice built in the seventeenth century. From there they look down on a broad panorama of rich fields and flourishing villages, lakes and rolling meadows, against a background of blue, wooded hills.

At length they go back and join the others at the tavern. Milena had several good friends among the artists, one of them being Staša's friend Hoffmeister, a caricaturist who was then working with Staša on a little book called *Happy Journey*. But as Milena had been away for years, she was meeting most of them for the first time; one of these was Karel Teige, the leading theoretician of a group of talented young architects, several of whom were now present. Nearly all were supporters of the Bauhaus in Dessau. The most gifted of them all was Jaromír Krejčár.

Everyone soon noticed that Jaromír had eyes and ears only for Milena. Of course he knew who she was. Everyone in Prague had heard of her, the new star of the *Národní Listy*. He had read her articles, particularly those on interior decoration. He knew they had similar tastes. They both favored a return to simplicity, and this was the first link between them. The years she had spent abroad gave Milena an aura of mystery. She talked about Vienna and Dresden. Jaromír listened, captivated by her beauty and intelligence. Afternoon turned to evening. The party took the last boat down the river. Songs were sung in the cool, starry night. After the Zlichov church the first lights of Prague appeared. On landing, the whole party went to the usual café of the Mánes group, near the somber Mill Tower, which protrudes into the Vltava like the prow of a ship. There was a chill in the air, and most of the excursionists ordered grog. But Milena had no need of a drink, she was drunk with happiness. She had fallen in love with Jaromír.

It was late when the party broke up. Jaromír took Milena home. Milena was afraid of a new love affair. But mightn't she for once do what everyone else did, toy with him, grant him "just this one night"? That proved impossible. Love crashed over them like a great wave. She married Jaromír in 1927 and the best years of her life followed. In his company, a new world opened up to Milena. Almost all the outstanding architects of the day frequented her house as well as leading figures of the modern movements in art and literature. Milena loved Jaromír's work. She was filled with enthusiastic interest in the revolutionary ideas of modern architecture.

Jaromír Krejčár, the son of a forester from Hundsheim in Lower Austria, had learned his profession from the bottom up. On completing his training as a mason, he attended secondary school in Prague, then building trades school, and finally the school of architecture at the Prague Academy of Fine Arts, where he studied the work of Le Corbusier, Gropius, Oud, Loos, Peret, Hannes Meyer, and many others. In 1922 he edited *Život (Life)*, the first journal of modern architecture to appear in Czechoslovakia. He took a special interest in Le Corbusier, whose greatness he can be said to have recognized sooner than his French compatriots. In 1923 Krejčár executed his first major project, the Olympia building, an eight-story reinforced-concrete structure. It was the first building of its kind in Prague and served as a model for many others. The Czech pavilion which he designed for the Paris Exhibition in 1937 and the Trenčín-Teplitz sanatorium in Slovakia earned him a worldwide reputation.

Jaromír's feeling for nature was different from Milena's. "When we walked in the woods together," she told me in Ravensbrück, "Jaromír became a different man, he was really a forester's son. We avoided the beaten paths and walked across country, he in

86

the lead; he had the supple, easy movements of a beautiful animal. The woods were his element. . . ."

It was during her time with Krejčár that Milena attained the peak of her productivity. In addition to her routine journalistic activity, she published three books between 1926 and 1928. In addition, she and her friend Staša edited the newly founded illustrated magazine *Pestrý Týden*, which they transformed into an avant-garde organ. Appearing in an unusually large format, it published excellent reproductions, ran outstanding articles on contemporary as well as historical topics, and altogether maintained a high standard. Probably too high for the general public. Sales were disappointing, and production costs rose steadily. After little more than a year, Milena and Staša were replaced by more businesslike editors.

Milena's first home with Jaromír was on Spálená Street, in a dull, ugly building, where Jaromír's widowed mother had a tiny candy shop, out of whose meager earnings she had financed her son's studies. Milena and Jaromír transformed an unattractive apartment into a charming home. It was simple in the Bauhaus manner, but despite indispensable modern conveniences, free from ultramodern coldness. When the alterations were complete, they invited their friends to a housewarming. One of the guests knelt at Milena's feet and declaimed, "Many thanks, Milena, for not transforming this apartment into a model of hygiene and antisepsis. . . ."

In Milena's memory her first years with Jaromír were a time of walking on air. Her marriage may have given her the only pure happiness she was ever to know, the happiness that comes of harmonious love.

She was expecting a child. To her that was the fulfillment of her love and life. But early in her pregnancy she felt ill and consulted a well-known physician, a colleague of her father's.

He listened sympathetically but did not think it necessary to examine her; he merely said in a fatherly, reassuring tone, "But my dear young lady, you mustn't be such a sissy. It will pass. . . ." Milena felt ashamed. Her condition did not improve, she was in constant pain, but she refused to see another doctor. In the eighth month of her pregnancy, Krejčár took her to a resort in the mountains, in the hope that she would recover in the bracing mountain air. To prove to Jaromír and herself that she was strong and not a sissy, she bathed in an icy mountain lake. Soon afterward she was taken with chills, fevers, and a kind of paralysis. She was brought back to Prague in an ambulance. The diagnosis was septicemia. The pain was excruciating. Krejčár notified her father, who came at once. His fears revived all the paternal love he had so long repressed. He never left her bedside, and to deaden her terrible pain he kept her constantly under morphine. A little girl was born, but Milena was too weak to take pleasure in the event. The doctors called in by her father gave her up for lost.

Milena expected to die and told her father so. After saying that Krejčár was hopelessly irresponsible and couldn't possibly take care of a child, Jan Jesensky asked Milena to have the baby given to him, Dr. Jesensky, the grandfather, to bring up. Milena replied without hesitation: "Rather than give you this child, dear Father, to make it as unhappy as you succeeded in making me, I'd have it thrown in the Vltava."

She did not die. She slowly recovered, but her left knee, affected by multiple metastases, gradually lost all flexibility. For fear of blood clots, the doctors hestitated to manipulate her leg. Her father, however, realizing that if more time was lost, Milena would be crippled for life, called in some specialists and suggested that they try to bend the leg under anesthetic. The experiment was successful. Jan Jesensky was so moved that he burst into tears and threw his arms around one of the doctors.

When Milena awoke from the anesthetic, she couldn't believe her eyes.

After more than a year of convalescence, Milena came home from the sanatorium with little Honza, her child. As long as she was lying in bed, she had hoped for complete recovery and had not fully realized how hard a blow fate had dealt her. Only when she began hobbling around on crutches and trying to resume a normal life, did she herself and others as well see how tragically she had changed. She had become addicted to morphine. Throughout her illness she had been treated with morphine, and now she could not do without it. She was a cripple. Before her illness, everyone had been charmed by her graceful walk; now one knee was stiff and deformed, and her walk was an ungainly limp. She had been slender and well proportioned, with fine features; now her face was bloated and shapeless.

Ten years later in Ravensbrück she looked back on those unhappy days. "What do healthy people know about the tortures that cripples go through! I couldn't have imagined—not even in my dreams—that I'd ever have a stiff leg." She felt that her illness and its consequences were punishment for the serene happiness of her years with Jaromír. "We have to pay for everything."

As we were passing the Gypsy barracks, we could hear their singing. I stopped, I wanted to listen to their sentimental songs, but Milena dragged me away. "I hate Gypsy music," she cried out. "I can't bear it. It always reminds me of the worst thing that ever happened to me. Jaromír and I had heard about the miraculous waters at Pieštany. We consulted a doctor and he thought mud baths might help my knee. So we went to Pieštany, and that's where the torture really began. After every bath they tried to bend my knee with some sort of orthopedic device. The pain was indescribable. Not only during the treatment but afterward, without interruption, day and night. To bear it, I needed more and more morphine. Jaromír, who had to buy it for me, was in despair. I began to despise myself. Where was my character? What had become of me? One day, I said to Jaromír, 'From now on I'm taking no more morphine. Don't give me any more. You must help me break the habit.'

"Neither he nor I had any suspicion of what happens when an addict is suddenly deprived of his drug. It wasn't just the horrible waves of pain. No, everything went wrong with my mind as well as my body. I'd lie writhing in my bed, and every night until late a Gypsy band would be playing in the bar downstairs. I thought I'd go mad. Those fiendish tunes made it a thousand times worse. One night I woke up in a daze. I looked for Jaromír. He wasn't there, but beside the lamp on the bedside table I saw a revolver. So that's what it had come to. Jaromír couldn't take any more, he couldn't stand me anymore, he was giving me a hint. . . . I lay there sobbing, and the Gypsy fiddles sobbed down below. . . ." Milena was silent for a while. Then a little more calmly, she said, "It's come to me lately that the revolver may have been a hallucination, maybe it wasn't there at all. But one way or the other, that was the end of my love for Jaromír."

A BLIND ALLEY

. . . it will be a foretaste of hell, of having to live my life over again but with the eyes of knowledge, and the worst will be awareness not of my obvious misdeeds but of those deeds that I formerly believed to be good. . . .

—KAFKA, *BRIEFE AN MILENA*

It took Milena a long time to recover her equilibrium. Her first attempt to repair her broken life led her into a blind alley. She became a Communist. In Ravensbrück she tried explaining to me how this had come about. She had been a superficial person up until then, taking only a marginal interest in social and political problems, and she claimed her illness had made her think. She believed that a crisis of this sort occurred in the life of every responsible individual. In the twenties and thirties any number of artists and intellectuals toyed with communism. But Milena would not have been Milena if she had not thrown herself body and soul into any cause she believed in. Still, the human values involved always meant far more to her than any political program.

Even before joining the party, she had stopped working for the bourgeois *Národní Listy* and taken over the woman's page of the liberal *Lidové Noviny*, published by Čapek and Ferdinand Peroutka. But her writing had lost much of its quality.

She was fighting desperately against her morphine addiction. Twice she entered a sanatorium of her own free will and underwent a detoxification cure. As her articles were almost entirely autobiographical, she wrote about her experience in the sanatorium. The second time she did this, her editor flew into a rage and bellowed, "My dear lady, this kind of thing must stop!" And stop it did in 1931, when Milena joined the Communist party.

At first she took her duties as a Communist very seriously. She participated in demonstrations and mass meetings, and felt that she was fighting for a better world. Her friend Josef Kodiček wrote at the time: "Anyone familiar with her radical temperament could guess that she would succumb sooner or later to the Communist fad. . . . But she soon recognized the lifeless, mechanical, inhuman character of Communism and in 1936 she was expelled from the party."

In the meantime she worked for the Communist newspaper *Tvorba*. Now in Ravensbrück she admitted to me that during her Communist period she had almost entirely lost her ability to write. After trying for a while to convince herself that the party held a monopoly on the truth, she soon wearied of rehashing the same old party slogans. She once went so far as to suggest—in jest or in earnest, it is hard to say—that *Tvorba* publish a humorous issue, standing the party line on its head, calling the Social Democrats brothers rather than enemies, and so on in the same vein. Comrade Julius Fučik, the editor in chief, almost had a stroke. Still, Milena's unorthodox ideas were tolerated for quite some time. One reason for this may have been the special character of the Czech party, which preserved a certain bohemianism that had long been banished from other Communist parties. Not so long ago it had even found room for Jaroslav Hašek—author of *The Good Soldier Schweik*, an anarchist, a joker, a man incapable of toeing any political line, who made fun of everything and everybody. And another reason for treating Milena with indulgence was that the party leadership may have hoped through her to gain access to the group of intellectuals surrounding her.

Milena's home life became more and more unhappy. Krejčár's infidelities gave rise to constant scenes. Neither he nor Milena was a very good manager. Surrounded as they were by a host of friends and hangers-on, money slipped through their fingers and they lived beyond their means, especially when Milena began to write exclusively for the Communist press, which brought in a maximum of eight hundred crowns a month. Added to all that was her drug addiction, which consumed enormous sums. Once, after a cure, she went straight from the sanatorium to the offices of the Social Democratic newspaper *Právo Lidu*, and asked to see Mr. Vaněk. Miloš Vaněk, the editor of *Právo Lidu*, was an old friend of hers. No, she could not give her name. She was still a member of the Communist party and did not want her party comrades to hear that she had been consorting with Social Democrats. After some discussion the porter let her in.

Miloš Vaněk was horrified at her appearance. She looked sick and unkempt, she was wearing a shabby man's overcoat and seemed deeply dejected. "I've just come from a detoxification cure," she announced. And then without transition: "Miloš, would you let me write for you? Could you take . . . ?" Then, changing the subject in midsentence: "Dear Miloš, please could you buy me a cup of coffee?" Of course he could. A moment later they were out in the street. Milena whisked Vaněk away from the big cafés and hurried him to a little restaurant in a gloomy side street. Clearly she wanted to avoid being seen. The coffee hadn't been ordered yet when Milena changed her mind. Could she have a pair of hot sausages? Of course she could. The sausages came and Milena wolfed them down. The poor girl must have been starving, Vaněk thought, and hastened to order four more pairs of sausages. Evidently Milena had not heard him give the order, for when the sausages were set before her, she flew into a rage and screamed at Miloš: "Are you trying to insult me? Have you forgotten that I'm a lady?" Miloš was only able to appease her by assuring her that he had ordered the sausages for himself.

From that time on Milena wrote for *Právo Lidu* under five different pseudonyms. As she didn't want to be seen at the paper's office, her articles were delivered to Vaněk by little Honza, her daughter. These articles caused him a good deal of trouble. Indignant at seeing their efforts rejected, various socialist ladies with literary ambitions demanded that Vaněk reveal the identity of these five mysterious contributors. But he held his tongue and continued to print Milena's articles, which were a lot livelier and better written than those of his party comrades.

One day in 1934 Peroutka, the editor of *Přítomnost*, asked Miloš Vaněk: "What would you think of a couple who claimed that they couldn't stay in Prague but absolutely had to move to the Soviet Union, because their child would soon be of school age, and the Prague schools were too bourgeois and corrupt?" This couple was Krejčár and Milena. Yes, they were actually planning to go to Moscow. Undoubtedly, the situation in Europe, the threat of National Socialist Germany, had something to do with it. Many intellectuals believed at the time that only the Soviet Union had the will and the power to withstand the rising tide of fascism. In their eagerness to "build socialism," quite a few of the architect friends of Jaromír and Milena had already gone to the Soviet Union, confident that they would find satisfying work. They dreamed of commissions to build housing developments, if not whole cities, and believed in the unlimited possibilities of the socialist state. Le Corbusier, Gropius, Hannes Meyer, May, and others had already gone.

Krejčár received an invitation from Moscow and went there

alone. At the last minute, Milena decided to stay in Prague with Honza.

The Soviet authorities commissioned Krejčár to build a convalescent home for workers and party functionaries in Kislovodsk in the Caucasus. He submitted plans. Much to his irritation he was asked to spend weeks and months discussing them with officials who knew nothing about architecture, but who kept raising two objections: Krejčár's style was too modern and his plans did not meet the requirements of life in a socialist state. In the end they were rejected out of hand.

Krejčár soon grew disgusted with Soviet communism and wrote disillusioned letters to his friends in Prague. No one but Milena answered. All his Communist colleagues dismissed his reports as vicious lies which did not deserve an answer.

As usual in Soviet Russia, an interpreter had been assigned to Krejčár; she proved to be a beautiful young Jewish Latvian named Riva, who had experienced the dark side of the Soviet dictatorship and spent time in prison. Krejčár and Riva fell in love. Inevitably they told each other what they really thought of conditions in the workers' fatherland.

After two years in the Soviet Union, Krejčár had not been able to carry out a single one of his architectural projects. All he wanted was to leave the country. He divorced Milena and married Riva, who actually succeeded in obtaining exit visas for them both, an achievement bordering on the miraculous in 1936, the year of the big Stalin purge.

Back in Prague, Jaromír Krejčár put up an impressive modern building on Palackého Vinohrady, in which, although he and Milena were divorced, he set aside a beautiful top-floor apartment for her and Honza. A balcony ran all around it, which she decorated lavishly with flowers. The apartment soon became known as "Milena's hanging gardens." At first the place was appallingly bare; as there was no money for furniture, they had to make do with a mattress, a few chairs, and some crates. But little by little, the "hanging gardens" became a model modern apartment.

Soon after Krejčár went to Moscow, the Communist party gave Milena a special assignment—to minister to a party member who had come down with tuberculosis. The party's motives were not purely humanitarian; the sick man was suspected of Trotskyism, and it was hoped that Milena would win him back to the party line. She found him lying helpless and emaciated in a dark basement room. She instantly forgot all about the party's instructions and resolved to do everything in her power to help him get well. And then something totally unexpected happened. Her patient fell in love with her. Milena could hardly believe it; how, she thought, could anyone fall in love with an ugly, crippled woman? This love, which she soon reciprocated, restored her lost sense of womanhood and gave her the strength to surmount the deep depression from which she had suffered since her illness. She heaped her lover with attentions, her devotion knew no bounds. Thanks to her loving care, he recovered his health and found a satisfactory job.

Milena's Communist episode was relatively brief. It was only in a state of confusion and weakness that she needed the support of a secular religion, and wishful thinking could not blunt her critical sense for long. Fortunately, something, perhaps her work as a free-lance journalist, had saved her from degenerating into a professional revolutionary. Still, she found it hard to break with the party and hesitated a long time before taking the final step. What finally decided her was the news of Stalin's first show trial that ended with the execution of Zinoviev and Kamenev. That was in the summer of 1936.

Unlike many other Communists, Milena was not crushed by her break with the party. She did not grieve for a lost god. Quite on the contrary, she was relieved to be free from party discipline. She soon recovered her creative talent and, thanks to the political experience acquired in the last five years, became a respected political journalist.

Several of her friends who left the party at the same time were less fortunate. Especially those whose whole life had been the party felt that the ground had been removed from under their feet. It was next to impossible for them to find their way back to normal life. Unable to live without political activity, many took refuge in left- (or right-) wing sectarianism.

One dismal, rainy spring day Milena was sitting with her friend Fredy Mayer in a dark wine bar in the heart of Prague. She spoke sadly of her past, of all the men who had played a part in her life. "It's been wonderful, it's been interesting, it's been exciting, but now I realize that it wasn't what I really wanted. I never really met the right man. . . . They talked too much, they were too neurotic, too impractical. . . . So many were afraid of life, and it was up to me to bolster them up. It should have been the other way around. I often dreamed of having a lot of children, of milking cows and minding geese, and having a husband who'd thrash me now and then. I'm really a Czech peasant woman at heart. The so-called intellectual strain in me is just an unfortunate accident." Fredy Mayer tried to protest: "Really, Milena, how can you . . . ?" She laughed aloud. "Yes, yes," she said, "I know that's not the whole story. But sometimes I can't help feeling that it is." And she went on in the same vein. In the end Fredy suggested that her whole experience could be summed up in the refrain of a song that the Prague cabaret performers Voskovec and Werich had sung. It is the plaint of an unmarried mother about the man who has deserted her after getting her with child. Each stanza ends with the refrain: "Men ain't human."

When she got home late that night, Milena found a bunch of

flowers waiting on the doorstep with a card saying, "Men ain't human."

For more than three years Hitler had been in power in Germany. In Czechoslovakia all those who were politically aware were observing developments with increasing alarm. In an article about plain people and their Sunday pleasures, Milena wrote: "One has the impression that even recreation is regimented, that people are no longer allowed to roam through the woods, tossing pine cones at tree trunks, making fires, pulling up poisonous mushrooms for the hell of it. In Germany the whole population marches out to the country on Sunday morning for their ration of fresh air and comes marching back in the evening, thoroughly out of breath. The little man from Slavland, dreamy, a vagabond at heart, humorous and disorganized, would creep into a ditch by the roadside and give way to fear like a child. . . ."*

*Milena Jesenská, "People in Movement."

11

NEW TASKS

As long as you keep climbing, there will be steps, they will grow under your climbing feet.

—KAFKA, *DER FÜRSPRECHER* (*THE ADVOCATE*)

A few days after Milena was expelled from the party, a young comrade by the name of Kurt Beer, who though still a party member was plagued by doubts, came to see her. She made it clear that she still stood for something that might be called communism but had nothing in common with what went by that name in the Soviet Union and in the party. "The Communists have ruined everything," she concluded. "Now we shall have to start all over again."

Though much older than Beer, Milena won his confidence by speaking to him without a trace of condescension, treating him as an equal, and listening to everything he had to say. From then on he became a regular visitor. Once she and her friends were discussing criteria of masculine beauty. Someone asked her if she knew any handsome men. "Závis Kalandra is handsome," she said, "especially his eyes, but what would his eyes be without all the wrinkles around them? Every little line in his face is alive. That's what makes it beautiful."

Once in the course of a violent political argument, Milena

flared up and said something deeply insulting to young Beer. His response was to walk out. He felt sure that this was the end of his friendship with Milena. That same evening she came to see him and apologized. No, "apologize" is not the right word. She had the gift of behaving in such a way that any harm she had done was not forgiven, but completely forgotten. It was not possible to "forgive" Milena. "You have a peculiarity," Kafka once wrote her, "I think it lies deep in your nature, and others are to blame if it is not always effective . . . this peculiarity is that you cannot make anyone suffer."*

In 1937 Ferdinand Peroutka, editor in chief of the liberal-democratic *Přítomnost* (*The Present*) and an outstanding journalist and man of letters, asked Milena to contribute to his journal. Both financially and in other respects, this was her salvation. *Přítomnost* was a political, literary, and scientific monthly, comparable in a way to the American *Nation*. Peroutka had known Milena for many years and thought highly of her writing ability. He thought her articles would give his rather solemn publication the light touch it needed.

Milena slowly got the feel of her new job. Her first contributions still showed traces of her Vienna fashion correspondence. Indeed, she took the opportunity to pay a belated homage to the city of Vienna, where she had spent so many difficult but also happy years. As long as she was writing for *Tribuna* or the *Národní Listy*, it would not have been possible for her to say anything pleasant about the former capital of the Austro-Hungarian Empire. In the liberal *Přítomnost* there was no objection.

Her first articles for *Přítomnost* were for the most part sociological studies full of compassion and humor, based on her thorough knowledge of Prague society. Every one of these is drawn from life. Once, while strolling through the streets, she caught sight of a sign: FRANTIŠEK LILIOM, GROCERIES. Memories

*Kafka, *Briefe an Milena*, pp. 151 ff.

of Molnár's play *Liliom*, of Vienna, the Prater, and the days of her youth poured in on her. She went to the nearest café and wrote a sort of farewell to Vienna.

"If you have never been in Vienna when the chestnut trees are in bloom and the whole city is fragrant with lilac, when in the Prater one swingboat booth opens after another; if you have never seen the greenish-gray light that the electric lamps throw on the leaves of the chestnut trees in the evening; if you have never seen the giant aspens on the banks of the Danube, never seen the vast violet-studded meadows with their ash trees and silver poplars that surround the Prater for miles around and on spring nights throw a chaste mantle over loving couples; if you have never strolled through the streets of the Prater of an evening, when gold and silver tinsel hops and sways on the fair booths and swingboats; if you have never heard ten different waltzes resounding at once from ten different barrel organs, and all that under a sky whose stars pale in the presence of so much glitter—well, in that case, you can't know who Liliom is, even if you've read Molnár.

"Liliom is the swingboat man. There's something utterly unreal about the amusement park at night. Like a stage. And next to every swingboat there's a man, a magnificent specimen from the Vienna slums, he's wearing a striped jersey and his cap is pushed over the back of his head. Paris has its apaches, though I don't know if they're authentic. The Vienna swingboat man is authentic all right. With a magnificent thrust of his powerful arms he pushes the boat into the sky. In it sit pale city girls, holding each other tight, the kind who only go out with their girlfriends on Sunday. . . . They look with wonder and adoration at the man who is flinging them into the sky with such magnificent vigor; but then they begin to be scared, they screech, their skirts balloon, and their carefully curled hair escapes from under their hats. . . . But what does it matter! They are borne high on a wave of unforeseen happiness, which the poor things have paid for with their hard-earned pennies. And the hero, in whose hands the coins disappear, who calls them 'Miss,' and says 'If you please' . . . the man with the glorious muscles, with the cigarette behind his ear, with the dirty hands, the flattened nose, and the crude, impudent sex appeal, the man who knows his way around and has no scruples about breaking the hearts of little housemaids and working girls—that man is Liliom.''*

Here the reminiscences of Vienna end, because her article isn't really about the Viennese Liliom but about František Liliom, the good Czech grocer. From that point on the article ceases to be lyrical. The Czech Liliom is a very different sort of man from his Viennese namesake. With deep sympathy and a surprising knowledge of the food industry, Milena goes on to describe the difficult and eminently useful existence of a small grocer in a big city.

In 1937 Milena asked Willi Schlamm, the editor of the Vienna *Weltbühne*, who had moved to Prague, to contribute to *Přítomnost*. He wrote his articles in German and she translated them into Czech. Not only this collaboration, but also the many tastes they shared—for music, literature, and laughter—soon led to a close friendship. Willi Schlamm was enormously impressed by Milena's capacity for work. She could squeeze sixty hours into a single day; she wrote, translated, did things for numerous people, kept house, and cooked for anyone who happened to be in the apartment. She never kept an appointment with Schlamm without bringing him some little present. She always had time. Busy as she was, she could sit calmly with Schlamm at the Café Bellevue near the Charles Bridge, where Schlamm did his writing, or she would arrange to have dinner with him in some little restaurant. She would always be in a mood for talking and laughing.

*Milena Jesenská, "František Liliom, Grocer," *Přítomnost*, December 15, 1937.

By 1937 she had thrown off all trace of her Communist past and freed herself from every sort of wishful thinking. She had the courage to denounce all threats to freedom, whether from the left or the right, whether from the Soviet or the National Socialist dictatorship. This even-handed attitude brought her into conflict with many antifascist intellectuals, who were closing their eyes to the reality of the Soviet Union. Milena had a gift for political prognosis. At the very start of the Second World War she said to friends, "If the Red Army were to liberate us, I'd have to commit suicide."

12

POLITICAL JOURNALIST

You have penetrating perception; but that in itself wouldn't amount to much, there are people running about the streets who invite such perception, but you have the courage of your perception and above all the courage to see beyond it, beyond that perception; seeing beyond is what matters most, and of that you are capable. . . .

—KAFKA, *BRIEFE AN MILENA*

Czechoslovakia was under increasing pressure from National Socialist Germany. In the course of 1937, the demands made by Konrad Henlein, the National Socialist leader of the Sudeten German party, became more and more exorbitant. In 1938, the crisis attained its climax when Henlein promulgated the so-called Karlsbad Program, providing for the full "legal" independence of the Sudeten German territory (northern Bohemia with its predominantly German population).

At the same time, it became evident that despite the defensive alliance concluded between France and Czechoslovakia in 1921, France and England had no intention of defending Czechoslovakia against Hitler. In May 1938 German troops were concentrated on the Bavarian and Saxon borders of Czechoslovakia. It was obvious that an invasion was planned. Prague reacted by massing its forces on the Czech side of the frontier with a speed and efficiency that can seldom have been equaled by any mo-bilization in history. This on the night of May 20, the day before the Czech municipal elections. There is reason to suppose that Hitler originally intended to invade Czechoslovakia on the twenty-first when the Czech security forces would be kept busy by the elections, though he later denied this to Chamberlain and ac-cused the Czechs of persecution mania.

Shortly before these agitated days in May, Milena went out into the provinces to report on the popular mood. She summed up her impressions in an article entitled "From a Bohemian Village."

"In this little village of roughly 700 souls some eight men were called up for a special military exercise. No one knew what had happened; all were sure it was war. They were not due to report for several hours, but fifteen minutes after receiving the order, they knocked at the schoolmaster's door: 'What are we waiting for? Come on, let's get going.' They had their reservists' shirts, their socks and underwear under their arms. They handed over their domestic responsibilities to their wives, and off they went. The schoolmaster wanted time to pack his bag, but what could he do in the face of such eagerness? There was still plenty of time, but he went with them all the same. One peasant was still in his potato field when his mobilization notice came. 'Hand me the soap, Mother, I'm off to the army,' he said, washed his hands and went.

"Their fighting spirit is marvelous. These quiet, peace-loving people wouldn't think of sidestepping their duty. Their courage is a matter of course. They are on their own soil, they want peace, good harvests and life, but they take up arms as casually as if they were going to lunch. No dramatic farewells and no patriotic songs. Hardly anyone in the village knew that eight men had gone. Within half an hour they had reported for duty. . . ."

At the end of the article, she speaks of an exemplary officer.

"I spoke to a man who had fought in the world war. He was not at all enthusiastic about soldiering and killing. The joints of his hands and feet were as knotted as tree roots, his face was like a weather-beaten stone. He told me how his officer had treated his men. He slept with them, ate with them, talked with them. You've got to remember that officers were a caste of their own, there's a world of difference between an officer and a common soldier: 'different tobacco, different pronunciation, white gloves,' as it says in the film *La Grande Illusion*. But our officers seem to have realized that our people needed officers who were soldiers before they were gentlemen. I don't know where that fine man's allegiance was, but I do know that he wrote letters for his men, because their horny hands had trouble holding a pen, and they were not very good at putting their feelings into words. He ate the same food (which wasn't bad, by the way) and smoked the same cigarettes. For two of his men he wrote a petition to clear up some difficulty with the tax collector. Without their knowledge he appended a recommendation and a request that the matter be expedited as much as possible. And, wonder of wonders, when the soldiers returned home, the matter had been settled to their satisfaction. Apparently it's possible to get things done without brutal orders and shouts of hurrah. I don't know if there are many such officers. But I do know that they are what's needed to make a good army.

"Our people won't need any prodding if the hour none of us is hoping for strikes. They will fight as a matter of course, as willingly as they responded to that mobilization order in May."*

The preparedness of the Czech people had its effect. After the May mobilization both the British and the French governments showed—for a short time, at least—a little more backbone. A spokesman of the French foreign ministry went so far as to say: "If German troops cross the Czech border, it will

*Milena Jesenská, "From a Bohemian Village," *Přítomnost*, 1938.

automatically trigger off a war, for France is prepared to give Czechoslovakia all the help it needs." But this spirit was short-lived and the danger was averted only for the moment. The firmness of the Allied governments gave way to new hesitations; because of their unforgivable ignorance of the National Socialist mentality, the Allied leaders were taken in by Hitler's solemn protestations. In the next few months the tension mounted. Henlein stepped up his demands and ended by categorically demanding the *Anschluss* of the Sudeten territory to the German Reich.

In panic fear of a war for which they were not at all prepared, the British and French governments implored the Czech government to make every possible concession to Hitler. In July 1938, it was decided that England alone should negotiate with Hitler on the problem of Czechoslovakia, the idea being that England would be able to take an "objective" view, since it was not bound by any treaty with Czechoslovakia. Without consulting the Prague government, Chamberlain sent a commission under Lord Runciman to Czechoslovakia to find out whether it was true, as Henlein and Hitler claimed, that the Czechs were terrorizing the German population of Czechoslovakia. Lord Runciman, who knew nothing about the situation in Czecho-slovakia, avoided any meeting with representatives of the Czech community and made no attempt to familiarize himself with the political, cultural, or social situation. He hobnobbed exclusively with the German aristocracy of Bohemia and crowned his mis-sion by meeting Konrad Henlein, the National Socialist leader, at the castle of Prince Max von Hohenlohe.

As a reporter for *Přítomnost*, Milena visited the frontier zones and observed the bitter hostility between Czech and German populations. This hatred often divided families. In one case, the husband was a German, the wife a Czech, and the children, lashed by nationalist propaganda, called their father an "enemy of his country" or despised their mother, who was boycotted by the whole village, as a traitor, because she had married a German. "Parents and children, husbands and wives, brothers and sisters threaten one another with, 'Just wait. It won't be long before we stop your mouths!' On the way to school, children call one another 'Czech whore,' 'Marxist pig!' and worse, or throw stones at one another. . . .

"Two people were killed in Eger. The Henlein crowd are saying openly—I've heard it myself—: 'We need a few more deaths, that will start the ball rolling.' They need martyrs. They need heroes. Two deaths aren't enough for them. . . . But it's no wonder those two were killed. With such a climate of bottomless hatred, boycott fever, organized terror, with this horrible situation in families, in factories, workshops, where all political or even national thinking has been swept away by psychopathic madness, it's a miracle if no one gets killed. Son draws knife against father, brother against brother. . . ."

In Eger, Milena met a German who was not a Nazi, not a supporter of Henlein. Forbidden to take part in sporting events and torchlight parades of the Sudeten German party, his children had become outcasts. "But," she writes, "even such parents don't dare explain to their children that they are Germans but not Nazis, because the schoolteachers tell their pupils to report everything they hear at home . . . and children vie with one another in spying on their parents. . . ."

In the next paragraph she deals with the situation of the Jews in northern Bohemia: "Now that Germany has gained in power and that power has been further inflated by propaganda, the Germans walk the earth like arrogant conquerors, claiming that their blood is better than other people's. In Germany the Jews have been uprooted, forbidden to work, deprived of their rights, and condemned to walk the earth full of fear and grief. They wander from frontier to frontier, nowhere finding a haven, worse off than in the ghetto, for there, though persecuted, they were at least together.

"There are not many Jews in the north of Czechoslovakia. Still, there was anti-Semitism even before the Nazis came to power. Today, it has come to the point that the few Jewish residents, for the most part businessmen, doctors and lawyers, hardly dare leave their houses. I have spoken to a doctor in Asch, who has lived there for twenty years. For miles around there is hardly anyone who has not gone to him with his ailments. Today everyone avoids him, people lower their eyes when they see him and cross the street to avoid having to greet him. He has hardly any patients left. When one does turn up, it is from far away. His daughter, now an adult, a cultivated woman, attended the local school; none of the other children would have anything to do with her. Later on, she made a friend. Her parents received the friend into their house as if she had been their own child. . . . Since March 13 of this year, this friend has stopped speaking to them. She didn't even bid the family good-bye. Yes, there are such people in the world today. The National Socialists undoubtedly regard them as honorable and heroic.

"In a small farming town near the German border, I learned the meaning of calumny. The rumor was spread that a young Jewish doctor was hiding a 'Communist arsenal.' No one stopped to ask where he could have kept it in a three-room apartment. Ridiculous as it was, the rumor spread like wildfire. From then on no one greeted him; when he entered a café everyone fell silent, the storekeepers waited on him grudgingly, making it clear that they could do without his trade. Calumny is a cruel weapon, more cruel than a dagger. When a man is murdered, he is taken to the cemetery, and there he can rest. A victim of calumny has to go on living, but his life is made unbearable.

"Henlein's paper *Der Kamerad* has a regular section devoted to denunciations like the following: 'We wish to report that the daughter of X, the mayor of such and such a town, has become engaged to a Jew.' 'Y, employed by such and such a firm, has bought matches in a shop belonging to the Jew Z.' Just these brief announcements without commentary. The names, of course, are given in full. The effect is immediate. The 'guilty' parties are systematically boycotted. Some people comply with the boycott out of political conviction, others for fear of being boycotted themselves.

"Such boycotts affect not only doctors, lawyers, and businessmen. With the cruel logic of all totalitarian measures, they also strike the poorest of the poor. There is a dressmaker living in the town of R. with her blind mother. She is German and Aryan. Sixteen years ago, a Jew had promised to marry her, got her with child, and abandoned her. Since then she had worked long days at her sewing machine and managed to bring up her child and feed three people. And then the proud Nordic race, with its heroic 'trample the weak' ideology, fell on the poor woman. Her 'offense,' for which she had been paying all her life, was discovered and revealed to the Nazi public. Since then, no one has given her any work, and her little boy, who had been serving as an apprentice artisan, has been dismissed. . . ."

Milena witnessed the increasing persecution of the local Jews even *before* the German occupation of Bohemia. She had no difficulty in imagining what their life would be when the Nazis took over. A year later, in March 1939 when all Czechoslovakia fell to Hitler, she knew one thing: It was her duty to help all those who were threatened, and the Jewish population most of all. And something else she had learned: Up until then she had thought of the army as a necessary evil. Now she awoke to the importance of national defense and came to look with new eyes on the Czech officers' corps, these representatives of a caste which had always been totally alien to her. In 1939, when Hitler occupied Czechoslovakia, it was she who recognized the political importance of saving at least a part of the well-trained Czech army, its officers and fliers, in order that they might contribute to the defense of England in the war that had become inevitable.

110

In this Milena demonstrated an almost prophetic clear-sightedness.

She also criticized the Prague government for its failure to deal intelligently with the German minority. In an article entitled "Germans against Germans—Czechs against Germans—and alas!—Czechs against Czechs,"* she describes the situation in the north. "The Czechs are boycotted by all—the only exception being the *democratic* Germans. But in the interest of the truth it must be admitted that no adequate attempt was made to build a democratic bloc including the democratic-minded Germans. The cardinal error of our propaganda and of the Czechs inhabiting the frontier zone was failure to understand that it was not yet too late to bolster up those elements in the German camp who, though speaking a different language from ours, shared our political outlook. . . . If that had been done, Hitler's propaganda may not have fallen on such fertile soil. . . .

"Wherever I go, the people are agreeable if I speak German to them. If you speak Czech, they shrug their shoulders and leave you standing. But once they see a Czech taking the trouble to talk German to them, they melt. I've tried it any number of times. The man in the street is touchingly grateful when he hears a Czech speaking German. His tight-lipped hostility evaporates. In nineteen cases out of twenty, he shrugs his shoulders and remarks with a friendly gesture: 'So why should we argue? You're a Czech, I'm a German. Let me live in peace and I'll let you live in peace.'

"And that's the crux of the matter. We should have realized sooner who these people are and what we wanted of them. If we had regarded them as German citizens of the Czechoslovakian Republic. . . ." Here the Czech censorship stepped in and cut seven lines out of Milena's article, a sign of the nervousness that

*Přítomnost, 1938.

111

had taken hold of the Czechoslovakian government. The article goes on: ". . . The Germans love their language, and I see no reason why we shouldn't respect that love. They are Germans but not Nazis. . . ." (Here the nervous censor stepped in again and deleted twelve lines.) "These people and their families," she goes on, "could have been carriers of democratic propaganda, they could have become ethical, social and cultural props of Czech democracy and of democracy as such in the north of our country. . . ."

After 1918 the government of the Czechoslovakian Republic tried to find a democratic solution to the problem of the German minority, but alas, they went about it too slowly, deterred by the anti-German feeling of the Czech population, carried over from the days when their country was a part of the Austro-Hungarian Empire. But it was not until 1933, with Hitler's seizure of power, that the problem became really acute. Hard hit by the world economic crisis of the thirties, the Sudeten Germans offered fertile soil to National Socialist propaganda. Though the seditious character of the Sudeten German party could not be held in doubt, President Masaryk, in the name of his democratic principles, refused to suppress it. In the general elections of 1935 Henlein won two-thirds of the German vote, and in 1938 the figure rose to 92 percent. Whatever historical or political reasons there may have been for the development of the crisis in the Sudeten German territory, the situation in 1938 was disastrous, as was made clear at the municipal elections of May 21, when the armed totalitarian enemy was on the borders.

Despite the menacing situation, Milena had not in the summer of 1938 given up hope that the Czech army and people would be able to resist Hitler. She failed to see that the battle was already lost.

With an excess of optimism, she concluded her article: *"One* thing is not in their [Henlein's party's] power: just what they most fervently hope for, namely, a repetition of what happened in Austria in 1938, the occupation without striking a blow, the Sieg-Heil promenade, the concentration camps, the banishment of masses of people from their country, the 'Jews, keep out' signs. In a word, they cannot possibly effect an *Anschluss.* . . ."

The attitude of France became more and more pusillanimous. It took only a slight push from outside to make the French government cave in completely. This push was provided in September 1938 by an article in *The Times* (London), inspired no doubt by the Chamberlain clique. It suggested that it might be better for Czechoslovakia to get rid of the border territories with foreign populations and thus become a homogeneous state. The writer of the article chose to forget that these border territories were bilingual, inhabited by Czechs as well as Germans. Soon after the appearance of this article, Chamberlain went to Berchtesgaden for a first conference with Hitler. England and France favored a settlement of the conflict, and that meant granting the Sudeten Germans self-determination. After these first concessions, there was no holding Hitler. On September 22, at the second meeting with Chamberlain at Bad Godesberg, his demands were so outrageous that in an access of courage even the defeatist representatives of the Western powers sent a secret warning to the Czechoslovakian government, advising it to prepare for resistance. This led to the second general mobilization of the Czechoslovakian army on September 22. The whole population heaved a sigh of relief and once again, exactly as in May, the men complied immediately with the mobilization order. That day there were demonstrations of joy in the streets of Prague. No one foresaw the tragedy that would descend unopposed on the Czech nation in a few days. At the Munich Conference on September 29, the betrayal of Czechoslovakia was consummated. With the consent of the French premier

Daladier and Chamberlain, in the presence of Mussolini, Hitler decreed that between October 1 and October 10 Czechoslovakia must cede to Germany those frontier regions of Bohemia, Moravia, and Silesia that were inhabited by Germans.

This was the beginning of the end. But in France and England it was greeted by rejoicing. Peace had been saved. . . . A wave of refugees swept across the new frontiers of Czechoslovakia. Thousands left the Sudeten territory, democratic Germans as well as Czechs and Jews. From Carpathian Ruthenia and Slovakia, which at the beginning of October declared their autonomy, came more refugees, seeking safety within the shrunken borders of Czechoslovakia.

In Munich, Chamberlain and Hitler had signed a nonaggression pact, supposedly guaranteeing the integrity of Czechoslovakia. It would be seen before long how seriously Hitler took this pact. In Munich he had become convinced of one thing: that where Czechoslovakia was concerned, Chamberlain and Daladier would put up with anything he demanded. Later he said of the two, "Our adversaries are worms. I saw them in Munich."*

Hitler regularly sent for the foreign minister of the Hácha government to give him orders. He put systematic pressure on Prague. The Hácha government resisted certain demands, but gave in to many others, such as the legalization of anti-Semitic agitation and authorization of a National Socialist party. The Sudeten German Kindt, a henchman of Henlein's, set himself up as the "Führer" of the 250,000 Germans living in Czechoslovakia, and did his best to influence the government on Hitler's behalf. A strict press censorship was introduced and almost all independent newspapers suppressed. The newly founded papers carried hysterical anti-Semitic propaganda and were scarcely distinguishable from the *Völkischer Beobachter*.

*The Nuremberg War Crimes Trial.

After the catastrophe of Munich and the betrayal of the Western powers, in whose good faith she had trusted, the tone of Milena's articles changed. As early as October 5, she drew up a calendar of the September events. This article is in a sense her master's thesis in political journalism. A week later, in "Beyond Our Strength," she drops all her old optimism and looks squarely at the crushing facts, admits that mutilated Bohemia can hardly hope for a future, but nevertheless tries to save what can be saved and to give good advice. To avoid despair, she stresses the few remaining positive factors and passes merciless judgment on the guilty parties, the Germans, the Western powers, and the opportunists in her own camp.

13

MATER MISERICORDIAE

For five long years, while Milena had belonged to the Communist party, her friend Wilma, like many other friends, had avoided her. No doubt this had been partly due to Wilma's own experience with the Communist party. Soon after 1933, Wilma had joined a Committee to Assist Refugees from Hitler Germany and thrown herself into the work with enthusiasm. The Czech Ministry of the Interior put the Mšeč castle at the committee's disposal as a home for the refugees. The ancient building with its enormous rooms, its yard-thick walls, and deep recesses was more like a dungeon than a place to live in. The committee was faced with the well-nigh hopeless task of converting the castle into a human habitation. Although the right-wing attitudes of the representatives of the ministry made for complications, it was possible to work with them, for Wilma and her colleagues stood by their guns and usually got their way. With difficulty they convinced the press and a part of the Czech public that even refugees were entitled to decent lodgings; they raised money wherever possible, and after grueling work, in which Dr. Alice Masaryk, director of the Czech Red Cross, gave generous help, succeeded in putting the castle into habitable shape.

But little by little Communists had wormed their way into the committee. To this no one had any objection, but before the "bourgeois" members realized what was happening, the

Communists began using the committee for their own purposes. Stubbornly and ruthlessly, they thrust aside those refugees who were most endangered but less valuable from the Communist point of view and soon gained absolute control over the committee. Only Communist refugees were lodged in the castle, and the committee was turned into an institution devoted solely to Communist interests. Wilma and those who shared her opinions looked on in helpless rage while the Communists took full control over the committee they had built up. Incapable of combating these ruthless and unscrupulous methods, one after another of them withdrew from the project.

Such had been Wilma's bitter experience when in 1937 she chanced to meet Staša in a train, and Staša told her about Milena's "Trotskyism" and her expulsion from the Communist party. Delighted at the news, Wilma longed to see Milena again. On her return to Prague, she called her up. Milena invited her over. Anxiously, Wilma stepped into the large apartment, wondering what had become of Milena in all these years and whether she had really broken with communism. Then she sat facing her on the airy terrace of the "hanging gardens," relieved to find that "nothing had changed. It was a strange thing with our friendship. Like the Moravian river Punkva, which is suddenly swallowed up by the earth, flows underground through caverns and grottoes, and rises to the surface somewhere else, as if it were an entirely different stream, so Milena would disappear for years; but when she rose to the surface, the same old sympathy revived, as if we had never parted. At every meeting I sensed that she was still the same and that our friendship was indestructible. . . .

"Hesitantly we revealed our disillusionment with the Communists, came to the same conclusions, and, filled with new sympathy, fell into each other's arms. . . ."

Wilma, who always stepped in where people needed her, had not let herself be discouraged by the perfidy of the Communists.

Along with several friends, she set up a new committee, which concerned itself chiefly with the increasingly numerous intellectuals among the refugees. On hearing about it, Milena showered her with questions, showing a passionate interest in every detail of the work. Unable to satisfy Milena's journalistic curiosity to the full, Wilma mentioned Mařka Schmolková, chairman of the Jewish Aid Committee, who was at the very center of refugee work and, Wilma felt sure, knew everything Milena wanted to know. Wilma had been friends with Mařka for years, and, in anticipation of Milena's meeting with her, she proceeded to tell Milena all about her.

Mařka had been born and bred in the same Old Town as Franz Kafka, and in a very similar atmosphere. Her mother owned a small dry-goods shop, in which Mařka, the youngest of the children, had helped after her father's death. She seemed to be a born shopkeeper. Then she married, but before long her husband died. It was only then that she began to take an interest in the problems of Judaism. She went to Palestine and returned a Zionist with a passionate interest in Zionist ideas and plans for the future. She had been given a thoroughly Czech upbringing and felt herself to be a Czech. But she was able to combine her Czech feeling with her fervent hopes for the Jewish people.

After 1933, when thousands of Jewish refugees poured in from Germany, Mařka Schmolková would make it her business to help them. Though retiring by nature, she soon found herself at the center of refugee relief work, and became a well-known figure both in Czechoslovakia and abroad. Up until then she had attached no importance to her appearance. How could she bother to think about clothes when the lives of thousands were at stake? But Mařka's friends disagreed. At length they prevailed on her to buy some fine material for a fashionable suit. The address of a tailor was found, and everything seemed in good order. Time passed, and in answer to her friends' questions Mařka assured them that the suit would be a masterpiece.

One day she appeared at a meeting in her new suit. Her friends gaped in horror. The suit had been totally bungled. "But no tailor could have done such a thing!" they cried. And Mařka replied with a shrewd smile: "Right! He's not a tailor. He's a housepainter." She had wanted to give one of her Jewish refugees a chance. A former housepainter, he had decided to learn the tailor's trade. To obtain his certificate, he was required to produce a "masterpiece." But no one would entrust him with a piece of goods for the purpose. So he had told Mařka his troubles. "What could I do?" she defended herself. "And besides, the goods were lying around the house. So I just let him have them. Isn't it a masterpiece?"

This story delighted Milena, and she was wildly enthusiastic about Mařka Schmolková even before meeting her. Wilma promised to bring about the meeting as soon as possible, but as they were all extremely busy, this took time.

Then one day the three of them met in the attractive rooms of the Společenský Klub. Wilma remembered this meeting as a great event. The two women were instantly drawn to each other, and as they were both keenly perceptive, each took note of the other's exceptional qualities: Both were distinguished by a remarkable gift of observation, by unusual quickness, and, perhaps most important of all, by the same love of humankind and the same passionate sense of justice. And last, not least, both had a fine sense of humor.

Beginning with the first cup of coffee, Wilma was treated to a dazzling display of eloquence, wit, and human warmth. As the conversation turned to the social and political problems of the day, it became evident that the two women shared the same deep sense of responsibility.

This meeting had a profound effect on Milena. It was then that she wrote "Ahasver [the Wandering Jew] in Weinberg Street," her first article about the fate of the Jews in 1938. Together, she and Mařka visited a refugee camp in southern Slovakia.

119

Under the impact of that experience Milena wrote: "Who is Mařka Schmolková? I made her acquaintance while I was writing my first article about refugees and looking for facts and figures. Mařka Schmolková lives in the Old Town of Prague, in a narrow little street that I hardly knew though I was born in Prague; she lives in a small, crooked house with a wooden stairway. But the moment I stepped in, I was enveloped by a wonderfully harmonious and cultivated atmosphere. The room contains any number of books, sculptures by Štursa, beautiful dark old furniture, and a telephone that never stops ringing. At first sight you would probably not call Mařka Schmolková pretty. Women who work from morning to night, who for years have lived face-to-face with the sufferings of others, are not likely to be pretty. But she is wonderfully beautiful. Something that comes from inside makes her face as strong and expressive as if it were carved from stone. Mařka Schmolková is personally acquainted with every refugee who has crossed our borders in the last few years. She knows his story, knows the danger he has been through. So much suffering has made her forget her own. She spends her life among the sick, carries on an existence between life and death, runs from office to office, from London to Paris, from Paris to Prague. She has visited refugee camps and has been in no-man's-land, that steamer packed with fugitives who after the occupation of Austria were admitted neither to Czechoslovakia nor to Hungary, and for two months lay at anchor on the Danube off Bratislava. Whichever way she looks, she sees only despair. Only occasionally, after tireless efforts, does she feel that she has accomplished something. But this woman has the admirable serenity that comes of faith.

"In September, when I was at my lowest ebb, I went to see her, intending to sit with her for just a little while. This woman emanates such tranquillity, such quiet good sense and courage, that the short hour I spent in her easy chair was among the most beautiful I have ever known.

"A good many women are engaged in so-called social work, but few are deserving of admiration. Mařka Schmolková is not a social worker, she is a champion of her people, whom she serves with the humble pride typical of its finest representatives.

"Years ago in Prague I saw the German film *No-Man's-Land*. No-man's-land is a term used in the First World War to denote the zone between the front lines, the strip of scorched earth between the trenches and barbed-wire entanglements of the contending armies. In the midst of a battle, four men, an Englishman, a German, a black American, and a French soldier who happens to be a Russian Jew, meet in this no-man's-land. Four terrified animals from the four corners of the earth, from widely different social classes, speaking different languages. In this film the Russian Jew is mute. The part was played by Sokolov, one of the greatest actors of the day, a man with a sad monkey face and typical Jewish eyes, those sad eyes that gaze out of past centuries upon the centuries to come . . . to my mind there was something prophetic about this character: the disheveled little Jew from no-man's-land, silent among talkers, a pariah among pariahs, his smiling eyes full of intelligence, heart and soul, fraught with the centuries-old suffering of his people—a man without a country, without a home, without a language. Mute indeed. I have heard of a rabbi who lives in Palestine and has stopped speaking any other language than Hebrew and does not let his family speak any other language. But sometimes at nightfall, he sits in the corner and hums tunes . . . the tunes of Russian songs. Palestine is his home and Hebrew is now his language. But Russia is his native land and its songs are Russian folk songs. Mothers, the village women, the men at work, the schoolchildren—all sang them. This man's soul was imprinted by his native land with all its sounds, habits, colors and shapes. He formed his ideas and his words in his native language. Then someone came and said: 'You have no business here. Go away.' The Jew left home and wandered and finally reached the Prom-

121

ised Land. Since then he has spoken only Hebrew and worn himself out working in a field which once again is not his own; he has worked hard and willingly, with his usual proud humility. But at nightfall in the corner of his room he softly hums his Russian songs. That is the mute Jew from no-man's-land.

"I saw the *No-Man's-Land* film years ago, but because the action took place before 1918 we fools believed all that to be a thing of the past. It left me feeling confident, convinced that all of us today were moving toward a free and radiant future. At that time we were still unaware of the strange twists and turns that history can take.

"Today there's a no-man's-land right behind the barn, only a stone's throw away. Between the German and the Czech borders—dear God, what a shameful border!—they have strung a length of wire across a field, put a barrier across the road, stretched a rope between the trees—a child could tear the whole thing down. It's a border that could bring tears to your eyes. And in some places a strip of no-man's-land has been left between the two borders. First the Czech army moved out; then came German (or Hungarian, or Polish) heroes and moved the Jews from the occupied territories into this strip of no-man's-land, then more Jews arrived from other occupied territories. Some came because they had been ordered to move here, others because they feared for their belongings, still others because they feared for their loved ones, who had remained in the occupied zones. The Czechs let them through their barbed wire, but they were not allowed to cross the German barbed wire. Nor were they allowed to cross back into Czechoslovakia. Yes, the barbed wire of 1938 is strong. One night some young Hungarian louts woke up a whole village and dragged the Jewish inhabitants—men, women and children—out of their homes, loaded them into trucks, drove them to no-man's-land, dropped them there and disappeared. At first there were only ten people, exposed to the cold in an open field. Then a hundred. Then a thousand. Much later and only after the British authorities had pledged that these Jews would emigrate and not become a public charge, they were given permission to cross into Czechoslovakia and stay with some Jewish families. All the time they were living in the open, in the wind, rain and bitter cold, they were fed by Jews who had not yet been driven from their homes. They came from far away to help. Czech, Slovak, even German peasants brought food.

"But how is it possible that human beings could force three hundred people, those in Bratislava, for instance, to sleep in an open field in the bitter cold? And this in the century of scientific progress and comfortable housing? Such things have been happening since the peace of Munich.

"A few examples: With his bare hands a father digs three pits in the hard clay of a field. In each hole he puts a child. Then he plaits three little roofs from corn husks and puts them over the pits. He himself sits on the ground nearby. If the people in the vicinity had not helped, the refugees would probably have starved. But they do come and help, they bring food, warm clothing, blankets, a tent, and an old moving van with a bit of straw on the floor to house the neediest: the man with gastric bleeding, the woman who is expecting a child in a few days, the woman who has already borne her baby in the open and wrapped it in rags someone had given her, the blind old man who is sitting on a pile of straw in the corner. . . .

"A Jewish doctor from Austria is running himself ragged, caring for these people. He was the first to receive permission to leave the camp and emigrate, but he only laughed: 'How could I possibly leave at a time like this?' And indeed he was the last to leave no-man's-land. He could be seen at all times running about in a shabby coat, and not for one moment did he lose his composure. When children came to him with frost-bitten fingers, he would say, 'Come, I'll put on some ointment.' And to the people from the aid committee, aghast at the sight of so much human misery, he explained comfortingly: 'It's not really as bad as it looks. Come, I'll show you around. . . . You'll get used to it. . . .'

"They lived like that for weeks. Today they have roofs over their heads. But on the Czech-Polish border 6,000 people are still waiting in no-man's-land. Some sort of temporary shacks have been put up for them. Soon they will all leave. Only the old and the sick will be left there to die. But the young and strong will emigrate. Next Christmas they will be living far away under roofs of their own. . . .

"It's not our fault that their lives are so hard in our country. As long as our own house was in one piece and hadn't been cut in half, we could be hospitable and helpful. The best we can do now is to wish them a good life somewhere else. And that we do with all our heart."*

Mařka Schmolková carried on with her work until the Gestapo arrested her three days after Hitler's entry into Prague. Before being arrested she spent hours at her fireplace burning papers connected with her protégés.

At first the Gestapo put her in a cell with criminals and prostitutes, thirty-three in all in a cell with four cots. Then she was taken to the Pankrac Prison in Prague. What happened next seems almost miraculous: The Czech authorities demanded her release, because the refugee problem was more than they could handle and they needed her help. Then they persuaded the Gestapo to send her to Paris to make arrangements for Jewish emigration.

Soon after her arrival in Paris, war broke out. Her road back was barred. It drove her to despair that she couldn't get back to her refugees. Instead, she crossed over to London, where she resumed her relief work. There she learned of the cruel per-

*Milena Jesenská, "No-man's-land," *Přítomnost*, December 12, 1938.

secution of the Jews in Germany and the German-occupied territories.

In March 1940 Wilma went to see her in her London office; Mařka had just received a letter bearing the news that her niece and former secretary, a woman in the prime of life, had been deported to Poland with her husband by the Gestapo. They were the first Jews to be deported from Czechoslovakia. Six million Jews from all Europe were to meet the same fate. Mařka read the letter and grasped its implications. She covered her face with her hands and for a long time sat silent. When she arose from her desk, she was a different woman. All the life had gone out of her. One morning a few days later she was found dead in her bed. The diagnosis was heart failure. Grief over the fate of her people had killed her.

14

LET US NOT PERISH...

Why can't we resign ourselves to the thought that to live in this very special, permanently suicidal tension is the right way (you used to say something of the sort now and then, and I tried to laugh at you). . . . That even here in the dark we can be so much alone is the strangest thing imaginable, and to tell you the truth I am able to believe it only half the time.

—KAFKA, *BRIEFE AN MILENA*

In the eyes of many Czechs the death of the Czech writer Karel Čapek on Christmas Day, 1938, symbolized the downfall of the Czechoslovakian Republic. Now that Tomáš Masaryk, founder and first president of the republic, was dead, Čapek, who had been his close friend, came to be regarded as the embodiment of Czech democracy. After the dismemberment of Czechoslovakia this laid him open to a torrent of slander, and these largely anonymous attacks, directed against the old democratic system that was so dear to his heart, wounded him to the quick. In "The Last Days of Karel Čapek," Milena wrote: "Karel Čapek had never been in perfect health. Sickly people love life and fear illness in a different way from the healthy. Their love of life is humble, as though they were further removed from it, as though they had had only a fleeting acquaintance with this glorious, magical thing. They feel life more intensely, and they see miraculous beauty in what others regard as commonplace. If trouble comes to them, their first reaction is one of humility. They say to themselves: It's probably as it should be, I can take it. Rather than bother anyone with their trouble, they crawl away into solitude. Their reaction to illness is not, like that of the strong and healthy, one of defiant rage. They withstand illness by refusing to pay attention to it; they shift it from their body to their mind and suffer it in secret.

"Karel Čapek doesn't seem to have taken to his bed until he was dying. Friends tell me how, when moving from his easy chair to his big bed, he would wave at a photograph of Tomáš Masaryk which he himself had taken and which was now hanging on the wall. He waved as people do from a train pulling out of the station. . . . Possibly this was no more than an involuntary movement. But who can say why it is that dying people, like animals, express the truth more forcefully in gestures than in words? I like to imagine, perhaps naively, that the dead writer took the picture of Masaryk with him and was still holding it when he knocked on the gates of Heaven.

"He lay down to die as a pious man does. I don't know whether Karel Čapek believed in God. But he was a religious man, a man with a carefully worked-out system of moral values. Like a landslide, the year 1938 had swept away everything that had seemed stable in the world. Blow followed blow. Lost was the friendship of France, lost was faith in the 'Marseillaise,' that hymn to democratic freedom, lost were mountains and frontiers; what remained was a paralyzed nation, the terrifying helplessness of the writer himself, and worst of all, the jarring new language spoken by many Czechs, who were fouling their own nest. This was too much calamity for the heart of a man like Karel Čapek, for whom to live was to build; for a man who loved a well-tended garden full of flowers, a hospitable house and the simple things of life. He was too modest, too diffident a man, to die of a broken heart. He died of pneumonia.

"While the doctors fought for his life, he spoke in calm and simple sentences. He asked, 'What's the weather like outside? Is there ice on the ground? In ninety-one days we'll go to Strž together. All of us. In Strž the trees and the grass will be green by then. In ninety-one days. . . .' "

Strž is a stone house in the Dombriš woods, not far from a dammed-up pond. It is surrounded by fifty acres of land. This land, this house and the view from it were as dear to Čapek's heart as if they had been living, breathing things. The more the world around him went to pieces, the more persistently he built. He moved boulders, regulated the flow of the brook, cleared ground. The result was miraculous: Those fifty acres contained everything that a man beloved of the Bohemian countryside could desire: ponds, a brook, a spring, a bit of a field, a copse, and a view of the intersecting lines of gentle hills—a landscape as harmonious as evening bells in the golden twilight.

"But there were too many days between Čapek and the springtime. He counted the hours and trembled, as though only the spring could save him. Ninety-one days. A ladder with ninety-one rungs. From the fourth he fell.

"On Christmas Day snow fell and his room was filled with blue and white shadows. For a long time he was silent. Then his color changed. His wife Olga came into the room. 'Haven't the doctors told you I was better?' Čapek asked. Those were the last words he ever said. At a quarter to seven he ceased to breathe. He didn't fight, he didn't struggle. He merely ceased to breathe, to live. Those who wish to can believe that he died of bronchitis and pneumonia."*

---

*Milena Jesenská, "The Last Days of Karel Čapek," *Přítomnost*, January 11, 1939.

When there was no other way of getting the material she needed for her articles, Milena took it directly from the enemy. In 1938 she obtained an interview with the press attaché at the German embassy in Prague, who was so taken in by her innocent, forthright manner that he supplied her with information unavailable to any other Czech journalist. But she never boasted of such success; it showed up only in her articles. At the embassy she made important observations. On her very first visit, she noticed that the embassy was literally swarming with personnel. She inferred quite correctly that the National Socialists were already planning an attack on Czechoslovakia and that these supernumerary "diplomats" were Hitler's "fifth column."

Even after the occupation of Czechoslovakia, Milena kept in touch with these representatives of the enemy. She wanted to see them firsthand, to study their mentality.

After Munich, Milena's influence on the policies of *Přítomnost* increased, for one thing because so many of her colleagues left—particularly the Jews among them, but also those who no longer dared express their opposition and those who preferred to keep still rather than compromise. In the dark autumn and winter months, she did not give in to the general feeling of hopelessness. The urgent need to provide help and consolation for those who were most endangered brought out a whole new set of talents in her.

In February 1939, four weeks before the Germans marched in, she replied to a provocative article by a German Nazi with a piece entitled "How to Handle the Czechs." Twenty-three years later an old man from Prague, who had been living abroad for years, read Milena's reply and was deeply moved. "How is it possible," he cried out, "that Frank [head of the Gestapo in Czechoslovakia] didn't have her arrested and shot?"

Milena was a master of camouflage, but in this article she threw caution to the winds. She flung the truth in the Nazi's face and turned his slogans against him. Most people today, especially the young, for whom the Hitler period is ancient history, who know Communist dictatorships only from hearsay and take freedom of the press for granted, will be unlikely to realize what courage it took in the Prague of 1939 to write such an article:

"A nation adapts psychologically to the political situation, and traces of such adaptation can be found in all of us. Our little nation of eight million people is developing a quality unsuspected elsewhere in Europe: an unusual variety of courage. Our courage takes the form of tenacity and endurance. The very fact that we have had to suffer more than fight may have sharpened our wits, has given each one of us the ability to size up a situation quickly. At first sight this may be taken for submissiveness. But such impressions are deceptive. The mere will to survive may not seem to be a very lofty idea. But thus far we have had no better. All we have ever wanted was to live in accordance with our nature and national character, speaking the language of our ancestors. . . .

"When I chance to look at photographs of these grandiose times, photographs of Berlin, Vienna, Rome, showing human walls, palisades of upraised right hands, forests of flags and streamers, marching columns under dazzling floodlights, I always think: that kind of thing could not happen here. I do not mean that we wouldn't be capable of organizing such festivities, I mean that such celebrations are alien to our nature. The Czechs have no feeling for legendary heroes. They are more concerned with simple, everyday matters. The closer a person is to us, the more we love him; the more simply and warmly he speaks to us, the more we welcome him. The fewer bodyguards he has, the safer he will be in our midst. This attitude has its roots in the profoundly democratic character of our people, in our need for human warmth, in our respect for the human individual and his absolutely free will, which to our way of thinking is the prerequisite of all true happiness. . . .

"We have often been told of late that we have been incorporated into the Greater German living space and that within this living space we constitute, so to speak, a country and a homeland.

"I am a Czech and as such I have a good musical ear. From the sound of a word I can infer its true meaning. 'Space' suggests sky, air, clouds, something vast, unconfined. But we live down here on the earth, on the soil from which we wrest our daily bread by our labor. We have lived here for centuries. Grandfathers have handed down their plows to fathers, fathers to sons. We have never acquired much 'space,' we are only a people of eight million souls, a people with its language, its manners and customs, its songs, its yearnings and ideals. In my opinion, we do not constitute a bridge between Germans and Slavs. We, the Czechs of today, constitute a bridge between the Czechs of yesterday and those of tomorrow. We shall teach our children the hymn of Saint Wenceslaus. That and nothing else. . . .

"A German National Socialist wrote in the last issue of *Přítomnost*: 'All Germans without exception are National Socialists . . . it is their self-evident right to proclaim their belief. . . .' I can only reply that we too demand nothing other than our self-evident right. . . . But when you write about the 'urgent need for a rebirth of the Czech soul,' I must repeat my question. How can a rebirth be urgently needed? A rebirth must be organic. It cannot be imposed from outside. No nation's soul can be reborn by command . . . the most that can be done is to paste on labels and speak of a 'successful rebirth.' If you get anything in this way, it will be a changeling. Just as the German soul required a period of slow growth before National Socialism with its rebarbative opinions could crystallize out, so the soul of the Czech nation grew slowly from the Battle of Lipany* to

*The Battle of Lipany in 1431, at which the Hussite army was defeated.

the battle of the White Mountain* and from then until Munich; and during this period of growth certain opinions have crystallized out, which pulsate like living things in each one of us.

"Our history can be summed up in two sentences, originating in two different epochs: 'Strike, kill, spare no time . . .'† and 'Don't let us, or those who come after us, perish. . . .'‡ Undoubtedly our present bears the mark of the latter. We may as well admit it. And take it as our duty to sing this song passionately and loudly—or merely to hum it softly. To these words we react at least as sensitively as the Germans to the Peace of Versailles. If you want to have us as good neighbors, you must honor this song, for it is the expression of our national soul!"§

---

*The Battle of the White Mountain in 1620, in which the Bohemian Protestants under King Frederick V were defeated, whereupon Bohemia ceased to be an independent country.
†From the war song of the Hussites, circa 1420.
‡From the hymn of Saint Wenceslaus, one of the oldest Christian hymns, circa A.D. 1000.
§Milena Jesenská, "How to Handle the Czechs," *Přítomnost*, February 15, 1939.

15

THE CATASTROPHE

Your earnestness and your strength—what depths they plumb!

—KAFKA, *BRIEFE AN MILENA*

On the night of March 14, 1939, Milena, like thousands of her compatriots, was unable to sleep. With despair in her heart she stood at her window, looking down on the familiar scene. The streetlamps cast the same shadows as on other nights, and the star-shaped square across the way was as deserted as usual. ". . . The only difference was that beginning at three o'clock more and more lights went on; next door, across the street, downstairs, upstairs, all along the street . . . meaning that everyone knew. . . . At four o'clock, the Czech radio begins to broadcast; every five minutes, the same brief announcements: 'Attention! Attention! The German army has crossed the border and is moving on Prague. Keep calm. Go to your work! Send your children to school! . . .' Over the rooftops a dreary dawn. A pale moon behind the clouds, faces drawn with sleeplessness, a pot of hot coffee, radio announcements at regular intervals. That is how great events creep up on us, quietly, unexpectedly. But once the thing has happened, we know we've been expecting it all along. . . ."

Milena shakes off her stupor, goes to the phone, and calls her

Jewish friends. Always the same question: "Have you heard?" And always the same answer: "Yes." She does her best to cheer them up. "Count on me. I won't let you down." "Milena seemed to have been made to deal with catastrophes," wrote Willy Haas, one of those she called up that night. "The more distraught her friends were, the more calm, the more steadfast, the greater she was."

At daybreak Milena went out to see what was going on. ". . . At half-past seven swarms of children were on their way to school as usual. Workers were on their way to their jobs as usual. The streetcars were packed as usual. Only the people were different. They stood there in silence. I have never heard so many people being so profoundly silent. No crowds formed. In the offices no one looked up from his desk. . . . At 9:35 the vanguard of Hitler's army reached the city center, German army trucks rumbled down Národní Třída, the main street of Old Prague. As usual, the sidewalks were full of people, but no one turned to look. . . . I can't explain how it came about that thousands of people suddenly behaved in exactly the same way, that so many hearts, quite unknown to one another, beat in the same rhythm. . . . The German army was welcomed only by the German population of Prague. . . ."*

A young German, Count Joachim von Zedtwitz, who had just completed his medical studies in Prague, has given an account of his reaction to the events of March 15. That morning, having slept through the entry of the German troops and suspecting nothing, he went out to buy rolls. The first thing that caught his eye was an army motorcycle with sidecar; a soldier in a foreign uniform was sitting in it. In a flash von Zedtwitz realized what had happened. His first impulse was to seize the man by

*Milena Jesenská, "Prague—On the Morning of March 15, 1939," *Přítomnost*, March 22, 1939.

134

the throat and choke him. But he restrained himself, for when he looked around he saw that the whole street was clogged with trucks carrying German soldiers, thousands of them, column after column. . . . Prague, the bastion of freedom, had fallen.

Tears were streaming down the faces of the people around him: Without a moment's hesitation he ran to the home of his Jewish friend Neumann, whose mother opened the door anxiously. Her son, she said, was not at home. What did Zedtwitz want of him? "How can you ask? You must all leave here at once." The old woman shook her head. "No, young man, we will never leave. The river is just behind the house. We know what to do."

To Zedtwitz such an attitude was incomprehensible. How could anyone think of suicide when it was time to band together, to fight, and to save those who were in danger? He ran from one Jewish family to another. At last he found his friend Neumann. "If you're ready to help," Neumann said, "I'll send you someone tomorrow. He will identify himself with a gray visiting card." Two days later Zedtwitz's doorbell rang. A tall, gangling Englishman handed him a scrap of gray wrapping paper with the name "Harold" scribbled on it. That was the beginning. A small group formed, including Harold Stovin, Kenneth Ogier, Bill Henson, and Mary Johnston, who until the day before had taught English at the British Institute in Prague. They were all friends of Neumann's. In Zedtwitz's opinion they were sensitive souls, unsuited to resistance work, but the arrival of the Germans and a sense of responsibility for the lives of endangered people transformed them into heroes.

Zedtwitz owned a car. Just what they needed to carry out their plan of smuggling prominent Jews across the Polish border. But while they were making arrangements they needed a hiding place for the fugitives, since the Gestapo was already offering high rewards to anyone providing information leading to the arrest of prominent Jews. Someone thought of Milena, who immediately declared her willingness to hide the fugitives in her apartment and participate in the group's work.

In an article of March 22, Milena wrote: "The German soldiers behaved decently. It is amazing what a change takes place when a monolithic formation breaks down the individuals, when one human individual stands face-to-face with another." She herself must have witnessed the following incident: "On Václavské Náměstí a Czech girl saw a group of German soldiers approaching. Because this was the second day of the occupation and everybody's nerves were on edge, and because on the second day we were able to think again and realize what had happened, she burst into tears. Then a strange thing happened. A German soldier, a common little footslogger, came up to her and said, 'Ach, Fräulein, it's not our fault. . . .' He comforted her as one comforts a child. He looked like a typical German with a freckled face and reddish hair. He was wearing a German uniform but was otherwise no different from one of our Czech boys, a plain man serving his country. Two human beings stood face-to-face and 'were not to blame.' Those terribly commonplace words are the key to the whole situation.

"The Tomb of the Unknown Soldier is on the Staroměstské Náměstí. On March 15 it was buried under a mass of snowdrops. . . . That strange force, which in some mysterious way guides our steps, had led swarms of people to this place, and they had laid armfuls of flowers on that little grave recalling great memories. The people round about were all in tears. Men, women and children. And once again their behavior was typically Czech: no loud sobs, no sign of fear, no violent outbursts. Only grief. Their grief had to find some outlet. . . .

"I caught sight of a German soldier at the back of the crowd. He raised his hand to his cap. He realized that these people were in tears because he was in Prague. . . .

136

"I recall our beautiful illusions and wonder if Germans and Czechs, Frenchmen and Russians will ever be able to live together in peace, without harming, without hating, without wronging one another. Will governments ever be able to settle matters peaceably as individuals do? Will peoples ever cease to be separated from one another by frontiers?

"What a fine thing that would be!"*

In this article, published by *Přítomnost* when the Gestapo had already made itself at home in Prague, Milena, ordinarily so unsentimental, was moved to pathos.

In the course of the months that followed the German invasion of her country, this brave journalist, who fought with her pen, became an active fighter against tyranny. On her advice, the group extended their list of people to be rescued to Czech officers and aviators. Milena's ingenuity, her gift for devising camouflage and finding hiding places, proved exceedingly useful to the rescue team, as did her look of innocence, her spontaneous charm, and her staunch impassivity under questioning by the police. To those very qualities which had formerly been criticized as immoral, numerous people now owed their salvation. Joachim von Zedtwitz, who now saw Milena almost every day, was impressed by her political sagacity. "At that time," he says, "Milena looked like Churchill. She had the same bulging forehead, the same prodigious intelligence in her eyes, the same asymmetrical mouth drawn in at the corners, the same look of determination. Her resemblance to Churchill is no accident; their looks reflected the same political genius." And Zedtwitz went so far as to say that her handwriting also showed her political gift, that with its heavy, almost parallel downstrokes and elaborate, elegant flourishes, it bore the mark of a passionate, many-sided nature, disciplined by an extreme effort of the will. About

*Milena Jesenská, "Prague—On the Morning of March 15, 1939."

137

her handwriting Max Brod wrote, "It shows, I believe, a certain resemblance to Thomas Mann's, and that is most unusual, for Thomas Mann's handwriting, especially in his early years, seems unique. . . ."*

Any journey to the Polish border at that time was exceedingly dangerous. One day young Zedtwitz's passengers were Rudolf Keller, editor in chief of the *Prager Tagblatt*, and Holosch of the *Prager Mittag*. They had driven only a short way eastward when the first incident occurred. Zedtwitz knew the Germans had set up checkpoints all around Prague, and yet, taking a corner at high speed, he drove straight into one. He barely had time to instruct his passengers: "Don't open your mouths. I'll do the talking." Thereupon, pretending that this was a routine check by traffic police, he jumped out, opened the hood, intent on distracting the German soldier, and pointed at the serial number of his engine. "When I saw the German soldier's face," Zedtwitz reports, "I felt sick. He had the look of a hardened criminal. But luckily he was slow on the uptake and my behavior threw him off. All he could think of saying, or rather snarling, was, 'Are you carrying a Browning?' " Zedtwitz snapped back in his best Prussian manner that he had no need of one. No further questions were asked.

They drove on. To avoid further checkpoints, they took back roads. All went well for a while. Then in Moravia it began to snow, and before long they got stuck in a snowdrift. At this point Holosch gave up; he somehow made his way to the nearest railroad station and returned to Prague. Rudolf Keller and Zedtwitz went on. They had an appointment to meet a guide in a certain village, but because of their delay he had already gone when they got there. Night was falling. Zedtwitz drove to a place where he hoped to find another guide. Leaving the car on

*Brod, *Franz Kafka, eine Biographie*, p. 278.

the road, he crept up to the house and knocked. A frightened old woman opened. "Take care," she whispered. "The man you are looking for has been arrested for smuggling people across the border." Zedtwitz hurried away. In the beam of his headlights he saw Keller standing in the road with a policeman. Mastering his fear, he joined them with a friendly "Good evening." The policeman turned to him and growled, "Papers!" To gain time, Zedtwitz took out an impressive sheaf of identification papers. But the law wasn't satisfied. "What about *his* papers?" "Don't worry," said Zedtwitz, "he'll find something." Slowly and deliberately Keller rummaged through his pockets. What he finally came up with was an Austrian certificate of citizenship issued in 1886. Keller was indeed sixty-eight years old. While the policeman was studying this document, Zedtwitz, fearing the worst, started improvising. "Good God, Uncle Rudi, how can you run around without papers at a time like this?" And then, to the policeman, in a confidential tone, "He'll never change. He still thinks the Emperor Francis Joseph is on the throne." Rudolf Keller caught on at once and played the role of a doddering old man to perfection. The policeman began to laugh. "All right. All right. But where are you going at this time of night?" Zedtwitz made up a long story about having to visit some dairy farms and losing their way. After a few jokes about senior citizens who couldn't keep up with the times, the policeman let them go.

There was nothing for it but to go back to Moravská Ostrava. They drove awhile in silence, then Keller asked Zedtwitz to stop, and said calmly, "Let me off here. I'll just lie down in the ditch and take poison. Why in God's name should a young man risk his life for an old man like me?" Zedtwitz replied, "There's plenty of time for taking poison. Let's have a good dinner first. Then we'll think it over." They came to an inn and ate a good dinner. Keller's spirits revived. Next day they found a new guide, who led Keller to safety in Poland.

On the day after the occupation the editors of *Přítomnost* met in a café to decide what was to be done. The situation seemed hopeless and all were deep in gloom. Milena was a little late. When she finally appeared, all looked up hopefully and one of the editors cried out, "Thank God, a man at last!" Much later Ferdinand Peroutka, the editor in chief, whom the Gestapo would arrest a few days later, was to remember a prophetic remark Milena had made while the Germans were marching in. "This is nothing," she had said, "just wait till the Russians get here."

When Peroutka was arrested, Milena took over the editorship and kept it when Peroutka was released two weeks later. He remained in the background, contenting himself with inspiring the most important articles and doing all he could to keep the journal from being suppressed for as long as possible. This of course called for the utmost caution. Some readers resented this "opportunism," and I can imagine that in the last months of Milena's journalistic activity a good deal of what she had to do must have gone against her grain. In one article she apologized, as it were, to the readers. Czech journalism, she wrote, was like a tree that had lost all its leaves except for two or three at the top. And dull-witted people, who didn't know how to read, were complaining that the tree had ceased to sound in the wind.

Milena did her best to smuggle hints and warnings into her articles. Little by little, they came to feature Czech nationalism. In part, this must have been dust in the eyes of the German censors, but in part no doubt it reflected Milena's conviction. She had always been cosmopolitan, but she was also a realist. She realized that in a country occupied by a foreign totalitarian dictatorship the only way of preserving the people's will to resist is to reinforce its national consciousness.

And there is yet another explanation for the milder tone of Milena's articles at the time. By concealing her real opinions from the Gestapo, it enabled her to carry on her relief work in relative safety.

But she did not content herself with legal journalism. She helped to found an underground organ titled *Vboj!* (*On with the Struggle!*) and contributed to other illegal organs. One day she ran into her old friend Miloš Vaněk in the street. They sat down on a bench; after a short exchange, Vaněk suggested that they put out an underground paper together. Milena burst out laughing. "Why not?" she said. "That will be the fourth."

A few days after Hitler's entry into Prague, one Herr von Wolmar was appointed to oversee the work of Mr. Smorane, head of the government press office. Smorane, an Agrarian, was a protégé of former Prime Minister Hodža; his opinions were far to the right, and he was no friend of Milena's. But he was a brave and upright man, and he succeeded for a time in playing a double game. In the end, he was unmasked by the Gestapo and executed.

A special sort of love-hate relationship seems to have developed between Milena and Herr von Wolmar. He summoned her to his office at least once a week and they had long arguments which they both seem to have enjoyed. She described von Wolmar as an intelligent, cultivated man with perfect manners. He always treated her courteously, never kept her waiting, and made her feel that he thought highly of her.

Only once did Herr von Wolmar lose his temper and forget his good manners. The occasion was an article of Milena's in *Přítomnost*, entitled (in German) "Soldaten wohnen auf den Kanonen."* In it she wrote that German soldiers' songs were much better, specifically, more "soldierly" than their Czech counterparts; this was because the Germans were a more warlike, more soldierly people than the Czechs, in whose songs girls and lilies

*Literally, "Soldiers Live Atop Their Guns."

of the valley figured more prominently than deeds of heroism.

Before writing this article, she had cast about for a typical German soldiers' song. Her friend Fredy Mayer, a German, suggested Bertolt Brecht's comically grisly song celebrating soldiers who live on top of their guns and make steak tartare of every foreign race they come across. Of course Fredy and Milena were well aware that this song came from *The Threepenny Opera* and was far from being a German soldiers' song. But they felt that this was something that a Czech woman journalist would not necessarily be expected to know. Milena jumped at the idea, and that was how the Communist Bert Brecht came to be published in *Přítomnost* under the Nazi occupation. But the matter did not end there.

All Czech-language articles were censored by Sudeten German Nazis, who had some knowledge of Czech but whose limited intelligence was unequal to the hidden allusions and subtle irony of Milena's articles. It never occurred to them that Czech readers might not take Milena's fulsome praise of German soldiers at its face value. Such passages as the following flattered their national pride: "Formerly, when a whole regiment of Czech soldiers marched past under our windows, the merry clip-clop of their steps sounded peacefully through the streets; today, when a single German soldier walks through a café, his firm tread makes the glasses ring and plaster fall from the ceiling. . . ." And she goes on: "The Germans are as well able to command as to obey. Their soldiers tremble in fear of their superiors and carry out orders without question. How very different, how utterly unsoldierly, were the Czech officers, who far from shouting at their subordinates, spoke kindly to them, until the soldiers realized that what was being asked of them made sense. . . ." This of course was pure irony. But the ignorant Nazi censors swallowed it hook, line, and sinker.

Not so Herr von Wolmar when Milena's article was brought to him in translation. He was intelligent enough to see through her little game. He sent for her and received her unsmilingly. "Tell me," he said, "did you ever hear German soldiers sing that song? Are you, or are you not, aware that it was written by the Communist Bertolt Brecht?" Milena played innocent. No, she didn't know. She had heard the song somewhere, she couldn't remember when or where. But she had never doubted for a moment that it was a German soldiers' song, because it sounded so very soldierly and so very German. By the time she concluded with a friendly smile, Herr von Wolmar's temper was at boiling point. He threw the pencil he had been toying with in her face and shouted, "Enough! There are limits to everything. Do you think I was born yesterday?"

That was a happy day for Milena. She was proud of having made this disciplined, cultivated German lose his self-control.

In every aspect of her life, in love, in friendship, her political activity, and her writing, Milena was a fanatic. Time and again, despite the increasing precariousness of her situation, this fanaticism drove her to state her opinions loudly and clearly. "In a time of political upheaval, with new political values in the making, Czech journalists have been the only mediators between events and people, the sole purveyors of the living word. Every one of us is conscious of this mission, every one of us realizes that to be a Czech journalist is today an honor." These remarks were addressed to her colleagues in June 1939. "In the present situation," she goes on, "we journalists are bound to share the same feelings. Anyone who feels differently ceased long ago to be worthy of his calling. . . . The rest of us have committed ourselves to the imperative mission of guiding the nation to new life, new hope and new tasks. . . ."

She attacks the German press and the letters in which German readers express the suspicion that the love for the Czech people that figures so prominently in her articles is simply an incitement to hate the Germans. "This suspicion is directed at all of us. Czech journalists, regardless of what paper we write for . . .

143

neither overtly nor between the lines has any of us ever suggested that one should proceed by stealth. . . . If we have to live side by side with the Germans, we must not allow our sense of national honor to be crushed. In cultural level, in manual skills, in industriousness, and in personal integrity, we are in no way inferior to the Germans. We are their equals.

"Never must we let inertia, discouragement or exhaustion impair this sense of our equality, which they deny. We have always said this and we shall continue to do so. None of us has whispered . . . none of us has so much as hinted that we should spy on the Germans, seek to ambush them. Undisciplined behavior, even of a purely personal nature, can destroy our whole nation. Each one of us proclaims loudly and clearly what is needed: stubborn endurance, courage and bravery; fear nothing, there is nothing to be afraid of; tell the truth.

"We are adults, cultivated Europeans; and every one of us is a thinking human being. . . . Czech journalists are neither bandits nor cowards. . . ."*

More and more, Milena's apartment became a secret meeting place and refuge. Sometimes as many as ten people were there at one time. The Englishmen would sit whispering in one corner; on the terrace a Russian Jewish woman would be playing with her child and Zedtwitz would be trying in vain to converse with her; Frau Menne, whose husband, the former editor of a newspaper in Essen, had already been smuggled across the border, was helping in the kitchen, and Walter Tschuppik, another German, who had been editor of the *Münchener Neueste Nachrichten* until 1933, was waiting patiently for his turn; meanwhile, Rudolf Steiner, who after successfully reaching Poland was chased back into Czechoslovakian territory by a drunken

*Milena Jesenská, "This Concerns Us All," *Přítomnost*, June 14, 1939.

Polish border guard, was running frantically from room to room, making pointless and dangerous phone calls. One day he went completely to pieces and announced that if he were not spirited out of the country at once he would go to the Gestapo and denounce them all.

Zedtwitz writes: "Milena, who always wore a blue dress and welcomed every new arrival with a sweeping gesture of hospitality, comforted them all. She did it just by being there. In her presence people felt and somehow behaved better."

Nevertheless Milena made countless mistakes. Her apartment was open to all comers; she talked too freely, neglected the most elementary precautions, and thought it necessary to make a show of her hostility to the fascist conquerors. She had no qualms about appearing on the street with her Jewish friends, and when it was reported that the National Socialists were forcing Polish Jews to wear a yellow star, she sewed a Star of David on her clothes and displayed it ostentatiously. She wanted to set an example and hoped her compatriots would follow suit.

Though she advised many friends and even her lover to emigrate, she herself categorically refused to leave the country and ignored all warnings. One of her friends told her what to expect if she was arrested. "Beatings," he said, "are hard enough to bear. But imagine what it would be like in a concentration camp if they pulled your hair out day after day. This's worse than being shot. . . ." Milena felt that she could not possibly run out on the people she had called upon to resist. It seems likely that she sacrificed herself deliberately, but she could not have suspected that the end would come so soon.

The Germans had not been in Prague for long when Milena's father called her on the phone. "Why," he asked her sternly, "haven't you been arrested yet? No self-respecting person should be out of jail at a time like this." What Milena said in answer is not known to us. But be that as it may, Jan Jesensky did not have long to wait.

145

The Gestapo had its eye on her. Soon she was summoned to her first interrogation. Asked whether she associated with many Jews, she replied, "Of course I do. Have you any objection?" Then: Where is your lover? No answer. He had left the country a long time ago. Next question: "Is the father of your child a Jew?" Reply: "I regret to say he is not." At this the interrogator lost his temper and bellowed, "That will do. We're not used to such answers here." "And I'm not used to such questions," Milena replied.

In June 1939, Milena was forbidden to publish, but she went on editing *Přítomnost* until August, when it was suppressed by the Gestapo. On September 1, two days before the declaration of the Second World War, Ferdinand Peroutka was arrested. Milena had gone to see him the previous evening. He was taken to the Buchenwald concentration camp. Some days later the collaborator Moravec, now minister of culture, had Peroutka brought back to Prague and moved to the fashionable Hotel Esplanade. After trying in vain to bribe him, Moravec thought he could force Peroutka to put out a National Socialist *Přítomnost*. When that too failed, Peroutka was handcuffed and taken back to Buchenwald, where he remained until the end of the war.

From then on, Milena felt the danger coming closer. Her main worry was what would become of little Honza if she were taken away. She was sorry to have drawn the child into resistance work. In the last few months Honza, an unusually intelligent child, had become a skillful conspirator, entrusted among other things with distributing illegal newspapers. Milena arranged with Fredy Mayer and his wife, whose daughter had just been sent to England with a group of children, that in case she was arrested the child would move in with them, but that if the Mayers, who were themselves in great danger, could not take her, they should hand her over to Milena's father.

One morning, about four weeks after Peroutka's arrest, Milena sent Honza to the printer's for copies of the illegal paper. When she got there, a Gestapo raid was in progress. Honza tried to clear herself by saying that she had just dropped in to use the telephone. When asked where she lived, she refused to answer. The Gestapo agents let her go and followed her to her mother's place. While they were searching the apartment, the little girl stood in one particular place and did not stir from the spot even when the Gestapo man hit her for not answering his questions. Pretending to be slightly feebleminded, she persisted in standing on a part of the floor under which some important documents were hidden. When the Gestapo men had finished searching the premises, they arrested Milena.

Honza lost no time in phoning the Mayers. They came for her at once, but she agreed to go with them only on condition that she could bring her best friend, a big black tomcat. He proved to be a difficult friend. He was not quite housebroken, and worse, he had the hair-raising habit of climbing out the window of the Mayers' top-floor apartment and strolling about on the roof. Despite the giddy height, Honza would climb out after him and plead with him to come back in. On one occasion, however, the troublesome animal won the respect of the whole family. The Gestapo had come to arrest Fredy. Three agents were rummaging in the cupboards and bookshelves when suddenly the cat jumped out of a dark corner, landed on the shoulder of one of them, and clawed him through his uniform. The men were so terrified that they broke off their search and led Fredy away without further ado.

Partly because of her precocious intelligence, Honza was a difficult child. Hardly a day passed without her causing some crisis. Often she came home very late and offered the most implausible explanations, most of them originating in her conspiratorial imagination: Some men had followed her, and she had escaped over long and devious ways and hidden in some house, where she had had to wait till nightfall before daring to come out. She managed to keep her foster parents in a constant state of alarm.

One morning the phone rang. "Gestapo speaking. Is little Honza there?" Frau Mayer, who was scared, stammered that she didn't know where the child was. "Too bad," was the answer, "because if you could get hold of her, she could go and see her mother at the Petschek Palace this morning. . . ." Needless to say, little Honza was found very quickly. Before setting out, she collected a big bundle of linen, in which she was determined to pack some secret documents for her mother. Despite her frantic resistance, the Mayers managed at the last minute to take the documents away from her.

In the spring of 1940, after Fredy had been twice arrested and twice released, the Mayers were obliged to give up their apartment and leave the country. In accordance with Milena's wishes, Honza was entrusted to her grandfather. When Professor Jesensky, that out-and-out anti-Semite, came to pick her up, he felt so grateful to Frau Mayer for taking care of the child for so long that he took her in his arms and kissed her.

Like all persons arrested for political reasons, Milena was sent to the Pankrac Prison in Prague, whence she was taken every morning to the Pečkarna for interrogation. This Petschek Palace, as the Germans called it, had formerly housed a bank. Its three underground levels, where the safes had been kept, were well suited to a Gestapo headquarters. Occasionally, Honza was given permission to visit her mother. Fredy Mayer would escort her to the Pečkarna until he too was arrested.

After many interrogations, which yielded little because of her skill at parrying questions, Milena was sent first to a camp at Benesov for persons who had consorted with Jews and then to a remand prison in Dresden. Here the damp cold of her cell and the starvation diet dealt her health a blow from which it never fully recovered. She suffered from articular rheumatism and lost forty pounds in next to no time. Almost a year later she was informed that the proceedings against her were being dropped for lack of evidence and that she was being brought back to Prague for discharge. In Pankrac Prison, however, instead of being set free, she was given a "protective arrest" order, providing that she was to be sent to Ravensbrück concentration camp.

Once again little Honza came to see her. Milena never forgot the sight of the long-legged child disappearing down the corridor beside the prison guard, striding self-confidently into a homeless, motherless world. Milena was never to see her child again.

At the end of October 1939—Milena had already been in prison for some weeks—the first student demonstrations against the German tyranny took place. A hundred and twenty students and schoolchildren were killed. On November 18 the National Socialists imposed martial law. Tens of thousands were arrested and sent to prisons or concentration camps. The persecution of the Jews was intensified from day to day. The Charles University of Prague and all institutions of higher learning were closed, first for a period of three years, then indefinitely.

16

A FREE WOMAN

Her eyes . . . reveal not so much the past as the future struggle. . . .

—FRANZ KAFKA, *DAS SCHLOSS (THE CASTLE)*

One might have thought that Milena would be persecuted by her fellow prisoners, because most of them, in their eagerness to adapt to their new life, played into the hands of the slave drivers. As a rule, strong characters who refused to submit were ostracized if not actually maltreated. Not so Milena. She was a surprising exception. She was persecuted only by the leading Communists, and that for political reasons. Yet there was something positively provocative in Milena's manner. Her way of speaking, of moving, of holding her head; with every gesture, she said, "I am a free woman." Though she wore exactly the same striped uniform as all the others, she stood out from among them; it was she who attracted all eyes. This might have antagonized her fellow inmates. The fact is that it did not. Here I am speaking not of Milena's many friends, but of the camp consensus. Her fellow inmates found flattering nicknames for her. Since the serial number she wore on her sleeve was 4714, they called her 4711 after the famous eau de cologne. As her married name was Krejcarova, her companions in Barracks No. 1 called her Carevna, or Empress. These little examples show

how her companions felt about her. In captivity, for some strange reason, one is drawn to some people and repelled by others from the very start. There is no doubt that in such a situation of hopelessness the weak are attracted to those who, like Milena, radiate strength.

Once Milena was late for roll call. This was a serious offense. The authorities might have turned a blind eye if she had hurried, which would at least have suggested a sense of guilt. But nothing of the kind, she blatantly took her time. An elderly SS overseer was so infuriated that she rushed at Milena, prepared to hit her in the face. Milena stood her ground and looked her straight in the eye. The woman dropped her arm and stood there open-mouthed.

Whether a prisoner was beaten or not often depended on her bearing. It can be said without exaggeration that a frightened, cringing look seemed to invite blows. "The funny thing about fear," said Milena, "is that it won't let you stand still. . . . When I stand still, it means that I'm calmly anticipating the unknown, I'm prepared for it." For that you have to be strong, and if you want to be strong, "you mustn't dissociate yourself from others, you mustn't forget that you're a member of a community. Once you feel alone, you start looking for a pretext to run away. Being alone is probably the world's greatest curse."*

Dr. Sonntag, the SS medical officer in charge of the infirmary, took an obvious interest in Milena as a woman. He treated her with marked politeness, tried to draw her into conversations, and once even offered her what was left of his breakfast, which she declined without thanks. He always carried a bamboo cane. When he wasn't posing with it, he used it to beat the prisoners. One day he stopped her in the corridor of the infirmary and tickled her under the chin with it. What followed took him totally by surprise. Milena grabbed the cane and flung it to one

*Milena Jesenská, "On the Art of Standing Still."

151

side along with the arm that was holding it. Her face, as she told me later, must have been flushed with anger and loathing. He didn't say a word, but from then on he made her feel his cold hatred. Yet surprisingly enough, he did not send her to the camp prison, as he might well have done.

Many of the criminals and asocials, even some of the political prisoners, were born toadies, glad to do anything that would please the SS. There was a German Communist woman, for instance, who worked in the tailor shop; she was responsible for shipping the finished SS uniforms and procuring the necessary material and equipment. She supervised a crew of prisoners, enforced strict discipline, and made such a good impression that the SS man in charge of the tailor shop once declared, "If I didn't have Wiedmaier, the whole shop would fall to pieces." We once asked her if she wasn't ashamed of herself, and she gave the astonishing answer: "I can't help it. That's the way I am. I'm conscientious, I have to work." It's true that in addition to satisfying her sense of duty, her conscientiousness brought her various privileges. She flatly rejected any idea of sabotaging the tailor shop. What did she care who the uniforms were for?

Olga Körner, a handsome white-haired old woman, worked at the assembly table, where parts of uniforms were fitted together before stitching. She too was a Communist and had been in custody for years. Unlike Maria Wiedmaier, she derived no advantage from her exhausting work, yet she too threw herself into it body and soul. Throughout the eleven-hour shift, she never sat still. She would run into the cutting room and argue endlessly with the overseers or SS men about matters concerning the cut of SS uniforms.

During my time in the tailor shop, at first I thought it was just by chance that I never heard her talking about anything but her work at the assembly table. But I soon realized that this was her whole world: pieces that didn't fit properly, mistakes

152

in the matching of camouflage colors, the careless work of the cutters, the praise or blame of SS men, her own tireless work and excellent results. Many of the Communists seemed to have been made for slave labor.

Milena had the same experience. The Communists working in the infirmary were always accusing her of laziness or—and this really showed how far they had sunk—malingering. "You're not sick," they said, "you just don't want to work."

The windows of Milena's office in the infirmary looked out on the compound. From her desk she could see the big iron gate that stood between us and freedom. Several women worked in that room. But the corner where she sat showed her personal touch. On her desk there was a flower in a container that looked something like a vase. Not to mention the glass button in the cardboard box where she kept her pencils. When the sun was shining, the colors of the rainbow appeared in it as though by enchantment. It didn't take much to delight us. On the wall by the window she had pinned a photograph of Prague and beside it a color print, undoubtedly taken from some SS calendar, showing a mountain landscape seen through an open window. What attracted us about this otherwise uninteresting picture was a white curtain billowing in the breeze. When you are yearning for freedom, a bit of curtain in a silly picture can make your heart overflow.

What images of freedom we carried with us into our captivity! Memories of books, of good music, films, popular songs, "tear-jerkers" which, as Milena confessed to me, she loved dearly. I had left Western Europe in 1935, and the more recent popular songs were unknown to me. I heard them for the first time in the camp. One of them had a special appeal for us: "The wind sang me a song, a song of unspeakable happiness . . ." Even now, forty years later, the tune carries me back to the first years of my friendship with Milena, to those unreal days when, pris-

153

oners among prisoners, we lived in a rich world of our own. Every gesture, every word, every smile, had its meaning. Constantly being separated and yet so close together, living always in anticipation of a brief meeting, even the bell of the little railway train running along the camp wall while we—Milena a few hundred yards away from me—were lined up for roll call seemed like a loving message from one to the other. In that existence without a future, we lived entirely for the present.

In a magazine that an SS man had left in the infirmary, Milena found a reproduction of Brueghel's *Return from the Hunt*. She cut it out and I pinned it to the wall of the orderly room in my barracks. Brueghel started us talking about the paintings we remembered.

"On my desk," Milena had written in one of her articles, "is a reproduction of a painting by Gauguin. It's in the corner, leaning against the wall. An enormous, boundless sky, below it the sea, and in the foreground three nude men on horses, two black and one white. They are riding through tall grass on their way to a water hole. It's a simple, economical picture, only a few lines, three human backs, three horses' backs with rippling muscles; it makes your heart ache. It tells of foreign lands, of an unknown sun, and a man who saw this world in such sweet colors: the sky a delicate pink, the sea azure blue, in the foreground three horses and three men, a sorrowful melody of colors.

"I love this picture not only because it is beautiful, not only because it tells me of the wide world and unknown countries, but also because it is a part of our world that I love so, a marvelous display of color, a cry of joy, a perfect expression of the universe. I found this picture in a small stationery shop, covered with dust in the showcase, and it only cost me ten crowns. But it has given me more pleasure than an expensive gift, a picture in a gilded frame. When I cease to take pleasure in it, I shall lock it up in my desk. If I come across it again

154

after a few months, it will awaken a feeling of past love, a sentimental memory of the day we spent together.

"At the bottom of my desk drawer there is a similar picture that I cut out of an illustrated magazine. It shows a man and a woman walking hand in hand on the seashore, into the sun and the wind. This picture is neither beautiful nor valuable; it's trash. Nevertheless, I shall never bring myself to throw it in the wastepaper basket. It brings back to me all the yearnings of a thirteen-year-old, all a little girl's wild ideas about life, and when I smile at it, I am smiling across the years of my adulthood at my own young girlhood."*

As I was physically stronger than Milena, it was only natural that I should try to take care of her. That sounds so simple, but with the strict camp regulations it involved considerable risk. All of us were tortured by hunger. But as those who like Milena were in poor physical condition suffered the most, I had no hesitation about stealing food for her from the kitchen. Actually I did the same for the women in my barracks. With the complicity of the young Polish woman who handed out the bread, I managed, thanks to a complicated system of miscounting, to filch several loaves of bread under the eyes of the SS overseer. Of course, considering that there were more than three hundred women in the barracks, this was a mere drop in the bucket. For Milena I managed to steal margarine from the kitchen in spite of the overseer who was standing right next to it. Milena, however, far surpassed me in daring. One morning during working hours, when the camp street was deserted, she carried a bowlful of coffee with milk and sugar—the gift of a Polish woman who worked in the kitchen—all the way from the infirmary to my barracks, taking care not to spill a single drop. If she had been caught, she would have been beaten and locked up in the camp prison, the dreaded *Bunker*.

*Milena Jesenská, *The Way to Simplicity*.

The combination of monotony and constant terror favored strong friendships among the inmates. Our prospects were as uncertain as if we had been shipwrecked on the high seas. The SS had absolute power over us, and every day could be our last. In this situation, we developed mental as well as physical faculties which tend to remain untapped in normal life. Under these circumstances the feeling that one was necessary to another human being was a source of supreme happiness, made life worth living, and gave one the strength to survive.

In October 1941, Anička Kvapilová, the young Czech woman who had formerly directed the music section of the Prague municipal library, was brought to Ravensbrück. Like everyone else, she had heard of Milena, but it was in the camp that they met for the first time. She was later to describe her first impression of Milena: "I was standing outside the infirmary with a group of newly arrived Czechs," she wrote. "We had been sent there for our medical examination. Depressed and bewildered by our first terrible impressions of the camp, we were anxiously awaiting the next torment. And then Milena stepped through the door, stopped on the stairs, smiled at us, and called out with a friendly gesture, 'Welcome, girls!' It came from the heart, as if, like a hostess receiving her friends, she was inviting every single one of us into her home. I was flabbergasted, I looked up at her and saw her shimmering red hair that surrounded her head like a halo. I'll never forget that impression. It was the first really human touch amid all that inhumanity."

17

"A TIME OF SADNESS IS RISING OVER THE HORIZON"

How naturally what's needed comes from you, always!

—KAFKA, *BRIEFE AN MILENA*

In the hot summer of 1941—the SS had introduced night shifts in the tailor shops—the undernourishment and weakness of the prisoners became increasingly evident. Their legs were swollen, covered with boils and abscesses. A few cases of paralysis were reported, possibly, we thought, brought on by Dr. Sonntag's syphilis therapy. Not until there were twelve cases was Camp Commander Kögel notified. There were violent scenes between him and Dr. Sonntag. Rumors reached the camp of a polio epidemic in the vicinity. Dr. Sonntag imposed a quarantine. The prisoners were confined to their barracks, no work was done, and no SS overseers were allowed inside the camp. At first prisoners were delighted but then the paralysis spread; every day more women were carried off on stretchers and placed in a special barracks. The victims all showed the same symptom: sudden inability to stir a muscle. But strangely enough, none of the "old" politicals were affected; most of the victims were asocials, Gypsies, and "Polack lovers," that is, German women convicted of "consorting" with foreigners. A week later, if I remember correctly, there were a hundred cases. I shall never forget the two weeks of quarantine. Glorious summer weather, deep-blue, cloudless skies. Except for two daily exercise periods the prisoners were confined to their barracks. Milena volunteered for service in the "paralytic shack," a punishment barracks enclosed in a barbed-wire fence, which had been evacuated for this purpose. Every afternoon, relying on the protection of my green armband, I made my way to it by a circuitous route. Milena would be expecting my visit; she came out to the gate, and we would sit on the ground with the fence between us. Blessed silence. No bellowing overseer, no barking dogs to disturb the peace. The camp seemed enchanted. Two woodlarks hopped about on the path not far from us, and from somewhere we heard the monotonous summer song of the yellowhammer. The air shimmered with the heat and smelled of sunbaked earth. Time stood still. It was the hour of Pan. Milena began to sing softly, a tender, sorrowful Czech song: "Oh, green hills that were mine. Oh, joy of my heart! It's a long time since I've heard birds sing. A time of sadness is rising over the horizon."

We spoke of past summers, of childhood vacations. "Do you remember how wonderful it felt when the summer breeze blew your thin dress against your bare legs? And the soft grass under your feet when we ran barefoot across the meadows?" Milena on Mount Spičak, and I not far from the Czech border, at my grandparents' house in the Fichtelgebirge. The same round hills in both places, the same dark pine trees and mountain meadows full of flowers. And now? I look at Milena's bare feet, perfect in their beauty, like a statue's. And now they have to hobble over the coke gravel of the camp street. It wrings my heart.

As I was leaving, Milena handed me a folded piece of paper through the fence. "Read this, then throw it away." This time it wasn't one of her usual notes, addressed to "my darling blue girl!" It was a fairy tale she had written for me: "The Princess and the Ink Blot." To get the feel of Milena's mother tongue, I had been learning Czech. Milena had to write. She couldn't resist a blank sheet of paper. For a while we exchanged letters every day. The paper was stolen from the office of the infirmary. We would reply "by return mail" during the next exercise period. Milena had a remarkable command of German; I was amazed at the richness of her vocabulary. Once she wrote a sort of preface to the book we were planning. I wanted to hide it, I couldn't bring myself to throw it away. But Milena insisted, and it was only when I realized that I would be endangering her as well as myself by keeping it that I finally destroyed it. Thus not a single line has been preserved of what Milena wrote in Ravensbrück. Once, when I told her how miserable this made me, she laughed and said, "I'll write it all over again as soon as we get out. It will be as easy and natural as peeing."

Milena wasn't always so optimistic about the future. Like all journalists, she hoped to write something better than newspaper articles someday. She felt she had it in her but feared that the opportunity might never come. "Do you think I'll ever accomplish anything?" she would ask me. "Or have I wasted my life to no purpose?" And she would add: "You have nothing to reproach yourself with. You've lived a full life, and that's more important than any scribbling. . . . How I envy people like your mother, raising five children. That is really a full life."

During the quiet quarantine weeks, we talked about poetry and prose. She deeply loved the poetry of her country, it had played an important part in her development. But when I told her how much poetry meant to me, she declared categorically that the age of poetry was over, that there could be no excuse for writing anything but disciplined prose; most of all she admired Kafka's prose.

After two weeks our blissful quarantine came to a sudden end. Another SS medical officer, a specialist, no doubt, came to Ravensbrück and lost no time in diagnosing mass hysteria. Dr. Sonntag was in disgrace. He avenged himself on his false "paralytics" by subjecting them to electric shock. The first batch were quick to jump up and go about their business. When the news got around, terror restored the remaining paralytics to good health. Only a few unfortunates, suffering from articular rheumatism or tertiary syphilis, failed to respond to this treatment.

In 1941 the first Ravensbrück "book" appeared. Conceived by Anička Kvapilová, it was dedicated to Milena. It was an anthology of remembered Czech poems, written in pencil on stolen paper and carefully bound in stolen toweling, colored with light-blue tailor's chalk.

But Anička did not stop there. She couldn't help it. She had to produce, though her literary activities put her in constant danger. She was the only prisoner to keep a diary and she collected the songs of all the nations represented in Ravensbrück. One of her most touching works was a little volume of Christmas songs in many languages, which she had heard the prisoners singing. The words and music of every single song were carefully inscribed and each song was decorated with a vignette. Her next work was entitled "Songbook for the Hungry"; it was a collection of recipes from all countries, lovingly bound in blue velvet stolen from the overseer of the SS private tailor shop, who had planned to make a new evening dress out of it.

In addition to her own writings, Anička collected those of the other Czech women. She kept them in a big cardboard box which she dragged around with her as a mother cat does her kittens. She kept having to find new hiding places for it, and it was the cause of a serious fight with Milena, who feared it would get her into serious trouble and wanted her to destroy it. But like many gentle souls, Anička was uncommonly obstinate. She never argued, she just quietly did what she pleased. She kept her box, and its contents grew. New artists appeared on the scene. Nina Jirśiková, a friend of Milena's, formerly a dancer and choreographer at the Prague Osvobozene Divadlo (Free Theater), discovered a talent for caricature. The result was the "Ravensbrück Fashions Magazine," a series of comic drawings. The first showed the new arrival, a lamentable figure with shorn head, wearing a long, striped sack-dress and enormous wooden clogs. The ensuing pictures embodied fashion hints for the demanding inmate. Shorten—secretly, of course, for it is strictly forbidden—the sack-dress. Take in the waist; here a few safety pins, filched wherever possible, will come in handy. Puff up the bust—here you will need all the resources of the dressmaker's art. Then you will be in fashion, your feminine morale will benefit. Further sketches illustrated the acme of Ravensbrück elegance, attained in 1943 when some of the inmates received parcels from outside. In conclusion the artist showed, side by side, a poor, bedraggled, parcel-less, "proletarian" prisoner and a supercilious representative of the "propertied class," dressed fit to kill.

Another of Nina's caricatures dealt with the struggle of each against all in the overcrowded barracks. In one sketch two hundred women are crowding around a small cast-iron stove, each trying to find a place for the soup she is trying to warm in a tin cup. A battle rages: Faces are convulsed with rage, one pushes another aside, the pile of cups on the stove totters and collapses.

Another sketch bears the caption: "I am in daily contact with the duchess." It shows an inmate climbing down from her upper bunk and putting her foot square on the face of the "duchess," who is lying in the next tier below.

18

PROTÉGÉES

I remember well one of Milena's numerous protégées, because I helped Milena to carry out her plan. This was Mischka Hispanska, a young Polish woman and a gifted painter. Her artistic talent was known to us from some of her drawings. She was a timid, delicate girl, and every day on outside work, hauling stones and shoveling sand, was a threat to her health. Out of regard for her talent, Milena resolved to help her, to make it possible for her to draw undisturbed. So she stole paper and pencil from the infirmary and forged an inside-duty card for her. My part of the plot was to hide Mischka in a corner of the Jehovah's Witnesses barracks. There she would sit at the window, doing bitterly realistic drawings of daily life in Ravensbrück and portraits of fellow inmates. Mischka, I felt, was in special danger because her propensity for self-pity seemed to invite illness.

The rhythm of our days was determined by the howling of a siren. It startled us out of our sleep in the morning, ordered us to roll call or to work, ordered us to fall in or fall out, and finally signaled the end of the camp day. We detested the "howler," as we called it. It was operated by one of the SS overseers; she alone had the right to press the button which was situated outside one of the three infirmary barracks. Several times I had heard Milena say, "How I'd love to press that button, just to see what would happen." I had imagination enough to describe the inevitable consequences, but that didn't discourage her. One morning she got up in the dark, crept over to my barracks, and whispered to me, "This time it's going to be me that makes everybody jump out of bed." A few minutes later the siren howled. I pulled the blankets up over my head and shook with laughter. That was typical of Milena. Just once she wanted to be "the flounder," as in the fairy tale of *The Fisherman and His Wife*. Actually there were no consequences, because no one imagined that a prisoner would dare to do such a thing. The SS overseer, the official button presser, said nothing, probably for fear that she had overslept and would be punished for it.

When deprived of their freedom, the weak often take flight from reality. Some began to live entirely in the past, spoke of nothing but their homes, and suffered from a kind of split personality which made it difficult or impossible for them to adapt to camp life. Others tried to escape the reality of the camp by reverting to childhood and behaving like irresponsible children. I was struck by the change in the inmates' reaction to horrible news. When the prisoners heard about death sentences and experimental operations, or about sick women being shipped to the gas chambers, their shock and consternation were short-lived; soon they would be laughing again or joking about the trivia of everyday life.

If a prisoner succeeded in adapting to camp life, in coming to terms with the loss of her freedom, her personality would undergo a slow change. The most dangerous stage, through which almost all prisoners passed, was resignation, acceptance of their fate. At this stage, prisoners lost their sense of solidarity and with it their self-respect and their hostility to their taskmasters. Some became submissive to the point of identifying themselves with the SS and became their willing tools. One of the most depressing aspects of concentration camp existence was the way certain prisoners came to revel in the exercise of power.

163

In a matter of days, prisoners given authority over others would change beyond recognition. Dejected victims became domineering, self-assured tyrants, who made life hell for their fellow prisoners.

In this third stage of concentration camp existence, the memory of freedom paled; one had to think hard to recapture it. When I thought of freedom, I still saw a grassy path through the woods, sprinkled with bright spots of sunlight. When I spoke of this to Milena one day, she said, "What an incurable girl scout you are. I am an inveterate city slicker. My idea of freedom is a little restaurant somewhere in the Old Town of Prague."

Some ten years before she ever saw the inside of a concentration camp Milena wrote in one of her articles, "I don't know who said that people were made better by suffering. But one thing I do know for sure: it's a lie." Ravensbrück confirmed her in this opinion. Most prisoners showed no sign of betterment, let alone ennoblement through suffering, and too much suffering could make beasts of them.

The asocials included numerous mental defectives, some of whom would not have been acceptable to any community, let alone a community of prisoners. One of these was a woman named Zipser, who was incapable of adapting to camp life and whose only response to her hopeless situation was hatred. She grumbled, she plotted, she denounced. Everyone, the SS as well as her fellow prisoners, hated and despised her. As a special humiliation, the SS assigned her to the cesspool gang, which was made up chiefly of Gypsies. On the very first day, Zipser, offended and angered by her demotion, picked a quarrel with the Gypsy women, who were total strangers to her. The Gypsies were not prostitutes, as she was, but passionate, spontaneous children of nature. Infuriated by her constant attacks, they soon avenged themselves in their own way. One day, they pushed her into the cesspool and held her under with poles until she suffocated. The SS overseer looked on without lifting a finger. Later on, when the crime became known, all the participants were arrested. Too much suffering had made murderers of these simple, primitive women.

But they were not the only ones who were transformed into monsters by camp life. Those with a sentimental, hypocritical streak were also susceptible, especially if they had power over others. Women who wanted to please everyone, including the SS, and were eager to make things as easy as possible for themselves, could easily become criminals.

In the political barracks there was a woman who had been taken into "protective custody" by the Gestapo for "malicious mischief." By gossip and defamation she had made enemies in the apartment house where she lived, including some National Socialists, who had denounced her, whereupon the Gestapo had sent her to Ravensbrück. But confinement did not improve her; on the contrary, it provided her with a rich field of activity. She came to be hated by everyone in her barracks, especially by the *Blockälteste*, a sentimental political with "a heart of gold." A *Blockälteste* had no easy time of it in any case, and if among her four hundred charges she had a troublemaker like this embittered old woman, it would have taken strong nerves and strong moral principles to make her overcome her personal dislike and treat the woman fairly. These qualities were lacking in her, and in the end, to make things easy for herself, she became an accessory to murder.

The old woman, who suffered from rheumatism and hated everyone, had only a small space in the barracks that she could call her own. This was her bunk with its straw tick. She took meticulous care of it, kept it spotlessly clean, and defended it against any encroachment. One morning she failed to get up. Since her companions ignored her, it was only when she soiled the tick she had taken such good care of that anyone noticed she was sick. Like thousands of prisoners, she suffered from

165

diarrhea. When it became known that she had soiled the floor on her way to the latrine, she was showered with abuse from all sides. Not a word of sympathy for the old woman's sufferings. Only hard words. And as far as her diminished strength permitted, she snapped back. The *Blockälteste* decided it was time to get rid of this "asocial element." She sent her to the infirmary. A hint to one of the assistants sufficed to have her given a lethal injection, thus ridding the barracks of her disturbing presence.

I can only wonder whether Milena, after her bitter experience in Ravensbrück, would have been so hopeful as to write, "I do not believe that hypocrites do better in life than forthright people, and I do not think the world is so evil that only the wicked can succeed in it."

In the infirmary, Milena kept the card file of the VD patients and gave them their pills. The greater number of them were asocials, prostitutes, or so-called "bed politicals," who had been arrested for cohabiting with foreigners. All the asocials were despised by the Ravensbrück authorities, and those with venereal disease were regarded as the scum of humanity. All, especially the syphilitics, could expect the worst. Dr. Sonntag used them as guinea pigs in his barbarous experiments, and many died. Samples of the new arrivals' blood were sent to Berlin for examination. The results came to Milena's office. Her courage and generosity can be appreciated only if it is taken into account that in the demoralizing concentration camp atmosphere there were few who saw fit to put themselves out for others, least of all for asocials. Since she regarded the asocials as neither more nor less than human beings in need of help, she had no compunctions about falsifying results and entering positive cases of syphilis as negative. In especially severe, infectious cases, she would arrange for surreptitious treatment. Every time she intervened in this way to wrest victims away from the SS, she risked her own life. If her forgeries had been discovered, she would have been lost. Not only did she do her best to save these women's lives, she also befriended the poor creatures, talked to them, and listened to their troubles. In many of them she discovered sparks of humanity.

Our friend Lotte, a German political, already had four years in prison behind her and was in very poor health. Milena knew that sufferers from tuberculosis were released from the camp. In the winter of 1942 she had a wild idea. She would help Lotte obtain a discharge. With her consent she put her name on a positive sputum specimen and had her moved to the tuberculosis ward. A certificate of discharge was duly made out and signed by Dr. Sonntag, and we all eagerly awaited the outcome. Every evening we stood by the window of the TB section and talked with Lotte. We already thought of her as a free woman.

We still had no suspicion of what had happened in the first months of 1942, or of the National Socialist plans to exterminate the unfit. An order came down to communicate the names of all congenital cripples, bed wetters, amputees, mental defectives, and sufferers from asthma and tuberculosis. The SS overseers assured us that they were being transferred to a camp where the work was easier. A medical commission actually appeared and passed the sick prisoners in review. Then one day two trucks came to take the first shipment away. That evening a horror-stricken Milena told me what she had seen. Patients had been brutally dragged from their beds and dumped into the straw at the bottom of the trucks. From that moment on she knew where those trucks were headed.

Two days later our worst fears were confirmed. The same trucks returned to Ravensbrück and stopped at the supply depot, where they unloaded a mound of miscellaneous articles: clothes marked with the serial numbers of the prisoners who had been taken away, false teeth, eyeglasses, a crutch, combs, toothbrushes, even soap. And there was our friend Lotte in the TB ward. Milena couldn't forgive herself. There was no time to be lost. She sent another sample of Lotte's sputum to be analyzed. And then another. Both of course were negative. Then she informed Dr. Sonntag of Lotte's miraculous recovery and implored him to discharge her from the TB ward. Luckily Lotte had worked in the infirmary and Dr. Sonntag knew her. That saved her.

One truckload after another left the camp and with gruesome regularity the clothing of those prisoners came back. When all those afflicted with "hereditary diseases" were disposed of, new lists were drawn up, this time covering all the Jewish prisoners. Milena and I saw only one possible explanation, yet, incredible as it may seem, our Jewish fellow prisoners with whom we discussed the lists, tried to convince us that they were only being taken to another camp. "Why would they kill us? That would be insane. Why would they want to kill strong young women who are still able to work?" One of the first to go was a young Jewish doctor, who promised to send us a message sewn into the hem of her prison garment. We found the note and read, "They've taken us to Dessau. We have to undress now. Goodbye."

Compared with the horror that now descended on us, the first year and a half in Ravensbrück had been almost idyllic. Polish women were summarily sentenced to death and shot. During the evening roll call, we would hear the shots from behind the camp wall. Adding to the terror, more and more experimental operations were performed, sick prisoners were put to death with massive injections of Evipal. Anyone who was weak or seriously ill lived in fear of being murdered. But it was not until the winter of 1945 that what had once been a "model camp" became a death factory. A gas chamber was built for, as an SS publication put it, the "eradication of all racially biologically inferior elements and the radical elimination of incorrigible political opposition which obstinately refuses to recognize the philosophical foundation of the National Socialist state."

19

THE ZEALOTS

Milena was one of the few who were incapable of becoming indifferent or letting their sensibilities be blunted. She saw the horror around her, she saw the misery, and it drove her to despair that there was so little she could do to help. Every evening she returned from the infirmary with gruesome tales to tell. She was a journalist and nothing escaped her. Despite the tension in which we lived, she never lost her ability to store up impressions. Perhaps it was her fear of violent death that sharpened her senses. Besides, we were determined to write our book, and for that it was necessary to cultivate our memories. There could be no question of closing our eyes, of shutting ourselves off.

Milena's health deteriorated. More and more often during the midday break, I would hide her in my barracks to give her a chance to rest. Lying down in the daytime was strictly forbidden. I could count on the solidarity of the Jehovah's Witnesses. But then came a harrowing incident which put an end to Milena's friendship with those sectarians. One day in the infirmary, she noticed the name of a woman from my barracks—Anna Lück—on an extermination list. Anna was suffering from glandular tuberculosis. For days I had been keeping her in the barracks, preventing her from going to the infirmary, for fear the doctor would order a lethal injection. But the doctor was already aware

169

of her condition. There seemed to be only one way of saving her. In a sense, the Jehovah's Witnesses were voluntary prisoners. They had only to sign a "declaration" that they were no longer Jehovah's Witnesses, and they would be released from camp that same day. I went to Anna's bed, told her what Milena had seen, and persuaded her to go to the office immediately and sign the "declaration." She got up and dressed while I disappeared into the orderly room so as not to attract the attention of the women who were cleaning the barracks, who would have tried to deter Anna Lück from this "betrayal," as they called it.

A little later there was a knock at the door and Ella Hempel, a member of the cleaning detail, stepped in. "Grete," she said with a look of hatred and revulsion, "I'd never have expected you to be in league with the devil. To make common cause with the SS. You advised Anna Lück to sign. How could you!"

Overcome with fury, I shouted at her, "Is that your idea of Christian charity? Sending your sister to the gas chambers in Jehovah's name! Cold-blooded beasts, that's what you are!"

When Milena heard about it, she flew into such a rage that the Jehovah's Witnesses lived in fear of her from then on. We discussed the utter intolerance of these people, their lack of sympathy for anyone who did not belong to their sect, and their cowardice when given an opportunity to perform an act of true Christianity. We came to the conclusion that they were very much like Communists. The only difference was that they worshiped Jehovah instead of Stalin. The Witnesses held secret Bible-study sessions in which they turned its content on its head to make it conform to their prophecies. The Communists gave secret indoctrination courses, in which they interpreted the news gleaned from Nazi papers—no others were available—in their own way, namely, as proof that black was white (or red) and that a Communist revolution was just around the corner. Milena's parallel between Communists and Jehovah's Witnesses

170

came to the ears of the Czech Communists, who from then on hated her more than ever.

Some time after the German invasion of the Soviet Union, the first large shipment of Russian prisoners arrived in Ravensbrück. In her eagerness to welcome the new arrivals, Palečková, leader of the Czech Communists and Milena's special enemy, volunteered for the bath and delousing team. What was said that day in the shower room I can only conjecture. The Czech Communist assured the Russian and Ukrainian women of the solidarity of their Communist sisters in Ravensbrück. It may have been then that she got her first taste of their profanity and abuse. Then she probably admonished them to show themselves, by their behavior in this German concentration camp, worthy of their Communist homeland. Like all the comrades, Palečková undoubtedly nourished high-flown illusions about these Russian women. Having benefited by a Communist education, what could they be but staunch supporters of the Bolshevik revolution? In reality, they proved to be a horde of undisciplined hooligans. Many were politically illiterate, and not a few expressed their hatred of the Stalinist regime in language that would have made a sailor blush. Palečková seems to have been profoundly shaken. She became sullen and taciturn. But for the present she continued to serve on the delousing squad. She told the women in the "old" politicals barracks that all Russians were not like the majority of the new arrivals. Soon afterward we heard that she was showing signs of mental derangement and that she often referred to Milena's parallel between Communists and Jehovah's Witnesses.

When Palečková's condition became clear to her comrades, they did their best to keep her from being taken to the infirmary, because the mentally deranged were invariably put to death. But they were powerless to save her. When an attempt was made to give her a sedative injection, she grew delirious. The medical officer sent her to the camp prison. The Jehovah's Witnesses

171

who worked there told me that her condition was hopeless: She refused to eat and stood with her back to the wall, crying out ecstatically, "Stalin, I love you." Two weeks later, a group of infirmary workers removed her dead body, which was little more than a skeleton.

A number of Communists worked in the infirmary. Day in, day out, Milena had to listen to their conversations. Their Communist jargon, their mouthing of slogans, threw her into a rage, and she was unable to hold her tongue. She was deeply repelled by the discrepancy between their words and their actions. They talked working-class solidarity, equality, brotherhood, in short, socialism, but their actions belied everything they said. What infuriated Milena most of all was their discriminatory treatment of the sick. They didn't ask: Are you in pain? Do you feel feverish? but: Are you, or are you not, a Communist party member? They distinguished between "worthwhile people," in other words "party comrades," whom it was important to save and for whom they did everything in their power, and the great mass of "worthless riffraff," who were not worth bothering about. This was too much for Milena's sense of justice, and she couldn't help giving them a piece of her mind.

She was quick to lose patience in those days and not only with her political enemies. Another thing that riled her was bourgeois sentimentality. Once when she was lying sick in her bunk, a Czech woman who had just had news of her daughter's wedding sat down beside her and gave her a long-winded report on the proceedings, not forgetting to mention her daughter's virginity, the bridal veil, the wedding night, and the importance of fidelity in marriage. When she had finished, she asked Milena for her opinion. Did she think her daughter's marriage would last, would she be happy, and so on? Thoroughly irritated, Milena replied, "The way I look at it is this: after her tenth man, your daughter may have learned something about the other

172

sex, so maybe she'll manage to live more or less happily with the eleventh."

All Communists indulge in wishful thinking, but in confinement their illusions get completely out of hand. They took it for granted that Hitler would be overthrown by a proletarian revolution and that resistance to national socialism in Germany was growing by leaps and bounds.

When Germany went to war against Russia, a wave of optimism swept over the political prisoners, and not only the Communists. Almost all were convinced that the Red Army would conquer, that Hitler would be overthrown, and that they would be liberated. Milena made no secret of her opinion. She resisted the general jubilation because she was able to think clearly and did not shrink from unpleasant conclusions. She was endowed with extraordinary political foresight, she knew what would happen if the Red Army overran Europe. To anyone who would listen she said frankly that if Stalin were victorious the West would forgive all his past crimes and give him a free hand for new ones. National socialism and communism, she said, were indistinguishable. In their premature rejoicing, the Communists let it be known that after the liberation Milena Jesenská and Margarete Buber-Neumann would be stood up against the wall by the Red Army.

After Palečková's death the leadership of the Czech Communists fell to Hilde Synková and Ilse Machová. It was they no doubt who sentenced us to death. But they were no more presumptuous than the Communist leadership of the other nationalities in the camp. All arrogated to themselves the right to pass judgment on everyone who disagreed with them, especially on "traitors," that is, former Communists, who in their eyes were even worse than "class enemies." Ilse Machová became Milena's special enemy. They had known each other in Prague. In Ravensbrück, Machová became a master of invective. And in other respects as well she showed the qualities needed for the exercise

173

of power in a Communist dictatorship. A Czech Social Democrat characterized her in a single sentence: "She's a chunk of rotten meat."

Milena thought with horror of the postwar period. She told me time and time again that Czechoslovakia would be granted only a few years of democracy. But she also thought it possible—though here I couldn't follow her—that her country would be handed over immediately to the victorious Stalin. "How can we escape the Russians?" she would ask. To comfort her, I thought up one escape plan after another; as she was too weak to walk, my plans always involved a lift in a car. Three years later I was to find out what it was like to be running away from the Russians.

Because of a serious infringement of the camp regulations I was moved out of the Jehovah's Witnesses barracks and Milena and I lost our refuge. In the summer of 1942 a gang of prisoners from the nearby men's camp put up a fence near the door of our barracks and dug a trench for new drainpipes behind it. The shutters on our barracks windows were nailed tight and we were threatened with severe punishment for any attempt to communicate with the male prisoners. All day long we heard their *Kapo* bellowing orders. We looked out through the cracks in the shutters. The men looked utterly miserable, and we were overcome with pity. Their striped clothing dangled from their emaciated bodies as from coat hangers. Only the *Kapo*, a common-law criminal, looked well fed. He had a club, and if any of the men wasn't working fast enough, he would get a violent blow in the legs. On the second day we began to communicate with the men. They were digging close to the barracks wall, and we whispered through the cracks. To all our questions they gave the same answer: "Give us bread." The sand had trickled away, leaving a hole under the temporary fence they had put up. We put bread into it. Then we stole margarine from the kitchen for them. Before long one of the men reported us. I was called to the office and questioned by Head Overseer Mandel.

Of course I told her that I knew nothing. Luckily for me, the same thing happened in another place, where I couldn't have been. But the suspicion was enough and I lost my post as *Blockälteste*.

As an "old" political, I was transferred to No. 1, where I lived under the same roof as Milena and slept in the bed next to hers. Every night as she fell on her bunk exhausted, she would sigh—the sound still rings in my ears—: "Oh, if only I could sit by the side of the road again and not be a soldier anymore!"

Once Milena said to me more in jest than in earnest, "Be horrid to me for once. It's so weird that we've never quarreled." Not long after that we had our first and last fight. One evening we were looking at a picture postcard, a reproduction of a brightly colored expressionist landscape that Milena had pasted on the wall beside her bed. I tried to explain certain details, interpreted spots of color as elements of landscape, discovered a mountain, a valley, and a lake. Milena contradicted me impatiently; she saw something entirely different. But I insisted on my interpretation. Suddenly she pulled the card down and tore it into little pieces. Her unexpected outburst upset me terribly and I burst into tears. Her panic-stricken reaction to my tears—"Don't cry! I implore you, stop crying!"—took away my last shred of composure, and I began to sob uncontrollably. But when I looked up and saw Milena's face, she seemed to be staring into the void. I stopped crying instantly and started talking, trying to pass the incident off as a trifle. But Milena said sadly, "It's awful to see someone you love crying. It makes me think of last farewells, of my tears in cold railroad stations, the heartless taillights of trains . . . the end of love. . . . Please, don't ever cry again. . . ."

But what could have made her so angry? I asked her, because to me it was incomprehensible, and what really startled me was Milena's answer. "All of a sudden," she said, "I had the impres-

175

sion that we had become like other people, who keep talking at cross-purposes as though there were a wall between them, I felt that nothing either of us said could reach the other's heart."

What made the usual torments of our days in camp, the interminable roll calls in every kind of weather, the commands, the blows and curses, harder to bear was the overcrowding which got worse from day to day. The Gestapo brought new prisoners from all the countries the Germans had occupied. There had long been more than ten thousand of us penned into a small area. The consequences were dirt, vermin, and epidemics. In No. 1 Barracks there were three women to every two straw ticks and in other barracks more; sometimes four women had to share a single bunk.

Milena and I took Tomy Kleinerová for our sleeping companion. Tomy, a friend of Milena's, was one of the unforgettable characters of Ravensbrück. In Prague she had worked with the YMCA; in the camp she became a street sweeper, armed with a broom and pail. I've never known anyone who could laugh so contagiously. She had an inexhaustible supply of jokes and anecdotes and even in the most hopeless situations she never lost her sense of humor. She had a bad hip that made it very hard for her to walk, yet she was never heard to complain. But then came news that her husband had been executed and that hit her hard. Her face went suddenly dead. It took her a long time to find her way back to life and laughter. At the liberation she went back to Prague and founded a club for war widows. At the same time she worked as secretary of the Association of Czech Resistance Fighters. That had disastrous consequences. Communists infiltrated the association and finally took over the leadership. Tomy resisted, but in the end they expelled her. In September 1949 the Communists took their revenge. She was arrested and in March 1950 sentenced to twenty-five years' imprisonment for "antistate activity, attempting to overthrow the people's democracy, and association with Anglo-American agents." For twelve years poor lame Tomy endured the hardship of a Czech prison before being pardoned in 1961.

I was working in the private garden of the SS administration when Milena had her first attack of nephritis. I found her lying in the infirmary, burning with fever and terrified of being killed with an injection. To cheer her up, we stole some gladioli in the garden and smuggled them into the infirmary under our clothes, flattening them against our emaciated bodies. Milena's pleasure was ample reward for our fear. She soon recovered, but from then on she bore the mark of her incurable illness and knew her strength was on the wane. She often complained that she had lost her capacity for spontaneous feeling, that her feelings had lost their freshness, become mere copies, memories of authentic feelings she had once had.

After her illness she would look at herself in the mirror. One day she said, "I look just like the sick monkey that begged for the organ-grinder who used to station himself outside my house. Whenever I passed, he would give me his cold little hand. Every time I saw him he looked more miserable. He'd give me a tortured look from under his silly little hat. . . . Those same sad eyes looked at me in the mirror today." And she concluded with a shrug: "Oh well, life is short, but death is long. . . ."

One day a group of male prisoners appeared in the corridor of the infirmary. They had been brought over from the men's camp to be X-rayed, for tuberculosis no doubt. The bulging feverish eyes of one of these skeletons looked familiar to Milena. She took the risk of walking past again and nodding to him. He nodded back, and she recognized the Czech historian Závis Kalandra, an old friend from Prague. Her discovery left her no peace, she felt she had to help him. There was an SS pharmacist who often came to the infirmary and also worked in the men's camp. He had a good reputation among the prisoners and Milena found an opportunity to speak to him and soon convinced herself that he felt sincerely sorry for the prisoners. He agreed to take a note from her to Kalandra. "Can I help you?" she wrote. "Do you need bread?" The note she received in answer said: "Milena, I beseech you for your sake and mine. Don't write again. You're risking our lives."

Unexpectedly Kalandra survived the German concentration camp and returned to Prague in 1945. There he was arrested by the Communists in 1949, sentenced to death, and executed.

20

FRIENDSHIP TO THE DEATH

Milena . . . who has learned time and again from her own experience that she can save another through her own existence and in no other way.

—KAFKA, *BRIEFE AN MILENA*

In October 1942, SS Senior Overseer Langefeld returned to Ravensbrück after a brief absence. She needed a secretary and I was chosen for the job. Prisoners with special skills, in my case stenography, typing, and a knowledge of Russian, were very much in demand. Langefeld knew me because of my work with the Jehovah's Witnesses. Milena and I thought it over at length. Might it not be wise to steer clear of this job? It was possible, because Langefeld for purely personal reasons chose not to contact me through the official employment office, which was directed by a high SS official. In the end we decided I should risk it, because the position offered opportunities for helping fellow prisoners. We underestimated the risks and had no way of knowing how badly it would end.

The prisoners thought well of Langefeld. She didn't bellow and she didn't resort to blows. She differed appreciably from most of her colleagues, who carried out orders mechanically and took brutal advantage of their power. Not all the women over-

179

seers and SS men in the concentration camps were evil by nature. I believe that one of the worst crimes of the dictatorship was to have corrupted average human beings and made them into its tools.

The SS needed more and more overseers to deal with the steadily increasing number of prisoners. Where volunteers were not forthcoming, recruiting campaigns were organized. An official from Ravensbrück would visit the Heinkel aircraft works, for example; a meeting of the woman workers would be called, and he would explain that overseers were needed for a "re-education camp" (the word "concentration" was carefully avoided). He would give a glowing account of the job: excellent working conditions, much better wages than they were getting at the factory, and so on. After each of these recruiting trips, some twenty young workingwomen would take up their new duties in Ravensbrück. Many were horrified when they found out what they had gotten into. They would come to Langefeld's office in tears and beg her to release them. But only the camp commander could do that, and most of the women were too shy to approach a high SS officer. So they stayed on. Assigned to a hardened overseer for instruction, they would look on as she meted out curses and blows. In addition, the camp commander would give them a kind of indoctrination course, explaining to them that the inmates were the scum of humanity and should be treated with extreme severity, that sympathy with them was unwarranted and contrary to camp regulations, and that any personal contact with the inmates would be punished severely. Only a few of the newcomers had sufficient strength of character to obtain their release. Most, however, were soon transformed into just such brutes as the veteran overseers. And yet, in the course of my five years of confinement I came across quite a few overseers who tried to remain human. One of these was Senior Overseer Langefeld.

It was only when I began to spend hours every day with her

in her office that I found out what she was really like. Confused, unhappy, unsure of herself. She soon began to talk to me, and listen to me, and in time I acquired a certain influence on her. In one conversation, or rather in her reaction to what I said, she put herself in my hands.

One morning when she came into the office, I could see she was seriously upset. She had had a bad dream. Would I interpret it? A squadron of bombers landed in Ravensbrück and instantly turned into tanks. Foreign soldiers climbed out and took possession of the camp. I am no expert at interpreting dreams, but to me the explanation seemed obvious. I replied without hesitation: "You're afraid Germany is going to lose the war." As a senior overseer, a member of the Waffen SS and of the National Socialist party, Langefeld ought to have had me arrested for that remark. But she did nothing of the kind. She gave me a horrified look but said nothing. After that I knew this woman would never do anything to harm me. And this had unfortunate consequences. I lost all feeling for the danger of my situation, and in trying to help my fellow prisoners involved myself in one breach of camp regulations after another.

Every evening Milena told me what had been going on in the infirmary and elsewhere in the camp. Dr. Sonntag had been replaced by Dr. Schiedlausky, Dr. Rosenthal, a Balt, and Dr. Oberhäuser, a woman. By their efforts, healthy women were turned into cripples, experimental operations were performed, and lethal injections were administered. Every morning Milena opened the coffins that had been placed in the infirmary yard. For some time she had been noticing corpses of patients who had not been murdered in the daytime but at night. She saw the marks of hypodermic needles, smashed ribs, bruised faces, and suspicious gaps in their teeth. As only one person was allowed to move about the infirmary at night—the patients were locked in their rooms—her suspicion fell on Gerda Quernheim, a nurse, who was also the *Kapo* of the infirmary. With the help of other infirmary workers, Milena got to the bottom of the grisly secret. Dr. Rosenthal was having an affair with Gerda Quernheim. He often spent the night in the infirmary, but not just to be with her. They would murder people together, and not only for the perverse pleasure of it. During the day they would select their victims, for the most part prisoners with gold teeth and gold crowns. Dr. Rosenthal would sell the gold in secret.

Pregnant women were sometimes brought to Ravensbrück. Until 1942, they were transferred to a maternity hospital for confinement, but from then on they were sent to the camp infirmary—a diabolical system, as soon became apparent. Gerda Quernheim functioned as midwife, and all the births were still-births. Once Milena distinctly heard the piercing scream of a newborn baby, and another helper, a German woman, opened the door from behind which it came. The newborn baby lay wriggling and full of life between its mother's legs. Gerda Quernheim had been busy elsewhere, and the baby had been born without her help. An unsuspecting prisoner had notified her, and a moment later the screams ceased. Gerda Quernheim murdered all the newborn babies, drowning them in a bucket of water. Ravensbrück was no place for new life.

Milena was horror-stricken. She told me about her discoveries and urged me to tell Langefeld about the nocturnal murders and the baby killing in the hope that she might intervene. After some hesitation I screwed up my courage and spoke to the senior overseer, who was shocked into a fit of hysteria and screamed at the top of her voice: "Those doctors are criminals. They're as bad as the camp commander." I could hardly believe my ears. "Is that what you really think?" I asked her. "Yes," she said, "that's what I really think." "In that case," I said, "how in God's name can you go on working here? Why don't you get out?"

Her answer astonished me. "But isn't it important for the

prisoners that I should stay here and try at least to prevent the worst?"

This I denied emphatically. I assured her that she couldn't prevent a thing, that they would go on murdering regardless of anything she could do. Nevertheless she stayed on. This woman still had a sense of good and evil, which her colleagues in the SS had long since thrown overboard. She had no illusions about conditions in Ravensbrück, but she wouldn't stand for any aspersions on the National Socialist leadership. Once she said in a tone of the deepest conviction, "Adolf Hitler and the Reichsführer SS [Himmler] have no idea what those scoundrels are doing in this camp."

Langefeld took a special interest in certain categories of prisoners, certain of the German politicals, the Jehovah's Witnesses, the Gypsies, and most especially the Polish politicals and the victims of experimental operations, most of whom in 1942 and 1943 were chosen from among Polish women who had been sentenced to death. Like everyone in the camp and the victims themselves, she believed that the operation earned the guinea pigs, as they were called, a pardon and that they would not be shot.

One morning in April 1943 a list of ten prisoners' numbers lay on Langefeld's desk. These were the numbers of Polish women who had been condemned to death. That meant execution. I sat at the typewriter with a heavy heart and looked out to see who these women were who were being taken to their death. They came around the corner, two of them on crutches. Without thinking, I cried out, "Good God, they're shooting the guinea pigs." Langefeld leaped to the window; a moment later she picked up the phone and called the camp commander. Did he have permission from Berlin to carry out death sentences on prisoners who had undergone experimental operations? Then she turned to me: "Go out and take those two guinea pigs back to their barracks." Her intervention saved the lives of seventy-five women who had been operated on. Its consequences for Langefeld and myself were less gratifying.

A few days later, on April 20, Langefeld had a brief telephone call, after which she rose from her desk. With trembling hands she picked up her cap and gloves. Then she came over to me and shook my hand, something she had never done before. Before leaving the room she turned to me and said, "I'm afraid for you. Ramdor is a beast."

I sat in the office alone, doing my best to control my agitation. Then, looking out of the window, I saw Milena approaching from the infirmary. What could she be doing on the street during working hours? Why would she be coming to the camp office of all places? Something terrible must have happened, something she had to tell me about, or she wouldn't have taken this risk. I ran down the corridor to meet her. "What has happened, Milena?" "Nothing at all. But suddenly I was so worried about you, I had to come and see if you were all right." I implored her to get back to the infirmary before anyone saw her. Just as she was moving reluctantly toward the door, Ramdor, the chief Gestapo official in Ravensbrück, rounded the corner, coming from the direction of the camp gate. "Get back into the office," Milena screamed at me. I rushed into the room and barely had time to sit down at the typewriter before the door burst open and Ramdor came in. "Buber," he ordered, "come with me!" As I stepped out of the building with him, Milena was standing motionless a few feet from the door. I'll never forget the look of consternation on her face.

Ramdor escorted me to the camp prison, the notorious *Bunker*. There Superintendent Binz took away my warm clothing and gave me light summer things in exchange. Then I was led barefoot down an iron stairway to a cell. The door slammed behind me. It was pitch-dark. Groping my way forward, I collided with a stool that was fastened to the floor. I sat down on it and looked about for light. I detected a faint glow under the door. I was too agitated to sit still for long. One soon learns to find one's way in the dark. Across from the stool there was a small folding table. Along the opposite wall there was a board. That was my bunk, but, as I soon found out, it was fastened to the wall and could not be used. In the left-hand corner beside the door were the toilet and a water faucet, and to the right of the door a cold radiator. Across from the door, high up in the wall, a barred window, hermetically sealed against light and air. The cell was four and a half paces long and two and a half paces wide. Back and forth I walked, back and forth, at first cautiously, knocking my shins against the stool, then more and more confidently.

Ramdor thinks he can get me down; well, he's got another think coming. How does he expect to do it? By keeping me in darkness? By starving me? How stupid of me not to have eaten all my bread that morning! Would they beat me? All the horrible stories I had heard about the *Bunker* passed through my mind. About prisoners who had been beaten to death, who had died of starvation, who had gone mad. My heart sank. I almost gave up hope. But then my courage returned, and one thought possessed me completely: Milena is outside. I mustn't leave her alone in the camp. Who will take care of her if her fever starts up again? If only she doesn't fall sick while I'm not there to help her! What if she should die! I heard her voice, I heard her moaning: "Oh, if only I could be dead without having to die. Don't let me die alone like an animal." As long as I was with her to comfort her, I thought she would get better and live to be free again. But here in the dark cell I saw clearly; I knew she was lost.

As I've described at length in my other book—about my three years in Siberian camps—what it's like to spend whole weeks hungry and freezing in a dark cell, I shall speak of it only briefly here. Just as a severely sick person welcomes the sounds of the new day after a night of suffering, so I welcomed the distant sound of the hated siren. I had got through the first night, but I had no idea how many more such nights would follow. I rubbed my cold hands, beat them against my body, jumped up and down to take the stiffness out of my joints, walked back and forth in my cage, searched for a trace of light, a sign of daybreak. But the darkness remained complete. Then suddenly my intent staring brought results. Wherever I looked I saw glittering balls and ribbons and stripes—a fascinating display which held my attention for a while and made me forget everything else.

But when I heard the first sounds from the corridor, I jumped up, rushed to the iron door, and pressed my eye to the little glass spy-hole. In vain. There was a lid over it on the outside. Footsteps approached. I held my breath, heard the rattling of tin plates, I heard the cell to the right of me being opened, and then the same sound on the left. My cell had been passed over. Had they forgotten me? I wanted to call out, to scream, but then I changed my mind, knowing that in this inferno nothing was done or left undone by mistake. Ramdor had chosen to soften me up for my impending interrogation by depriving me of food and light, by leaving me to lie on the cold floor without a blanket.

After five years of confinement in prisons and camps, after the horrors of Siberia, I was more resistant than some of the others who were suffering the same torment in the neighboring cells. I didn't scream, I didn't weep, I didn't hammer the iron door with my fists, I repressed all self-pity, because I needed my strength, I had to survive for Milena's sake. But when the body is weakened, the strongest character ceases to be an impregnable fortress. After the second sleepless night, shivering with the cold and tortured by gnawing hunger, my mind would cloud over from time to time. I saw loaves of bread piled up around me, I would reach out and then . . . a cruel awakening! Once that day the light went on, I heard the lid of the spy-hole being lifted; they were watching me, observing my reactions.

186

Someone was taking pleasure in my weakness. What a ghastly thought! Wanting to hide my face from those eyes, I crept into the corner behind the toilet and hid my head.

I lost all sense of time. One hallucination followed another. All around me I saw big platters piled high with macaroni. I would bend over as greedily as a hungry animal. Every time my head would collide with the cold stone of the toilet bowl. But the torments of hunger soon passed, giving way to an overpowering desire for warmth. The cell was full of silky, downy quilts, but whenever I tried to pull one over me, my merciful unconsciousness was shattered. And then I stopped feeling cold. All sensation went out of me. All I felt was a faint pulse beat in my throat. And phosphorescent figures moved through the darkness, approached me, bent protectively over me and vanished. An endless procession. A great sense of peace came over me.

The angry voice of the SS overseer shocked me into consciousness: "Hey there! Don't you want your bread?" I crept to the door and took the bread ration and the mug of hot ersatz coffee. That was on the morning of my seventh day in the cell. With the first swallow of hot coffee, the first mouthful of black bread, my desire to live revived. I broke the bread into three equal chunks and ate only one of them. There would surely be tomorrows and it was best to take my precautions. This was the seventh day; from then on I was given the regular camp ration every four days—a cruel rhythm, subtle torture, a kind of semi-starvation. The midday meal consisted of five potatoes cooked in their skins with a little vegetable sauce. I had the courage to put three of them aside, one of which I ate on each of the foodless days.

Even in the darkness of the cell every minute had to be lived through. I distinguished day from night by a faint glimmer under the door. I sat huddled on the floor, staring at the thin strip of light; I crept closer and closer to it, and in the end I lay flat, pressing my lips to that faint vestige of beloved daylight.

187

When you live in perpetual darkness, your sense of hearing gradually takes over from your eyesight. The concrete *Bunker* had about a hundred cells, arranged in two tiers around a court. Acoustically it was like a swimming pool. I was soon able to differentiate the various outside sounds, to tell exactly from what direction and from how far away an overseer's scolding or a prisoner's sobs were coming. Beatings were dealt out on Fridays in a special room. In 1940 Himmler had introduced this type of punishment for women. Such offenses as theft, refusal to work, and lesbianism were punished by twenty-five, fifty, or seventy-five strokes. Any German woman convicted of sexual relations with a foreigner was punished with twenty-five strokes in addition to having her head shaved. The screams of the victims resounded through the building. It did no good to stop my ears; I heard it all the same, heard it with my skin, with my whole body; the pain went to my heart.

Two Jehovah's Witnesses, whom I knew well, worked as cleaning women in the *Bunker*. Every morning the light went on and a Witness with a livid, expressionless face would hand me a dustpan and brush to clean my cell with. The corners of her mouth were drawn down in a mask of sympathy. A few minutes later she would come back for her dustpan and brush. Then, before I had time to say a word, to ask her for a piece of bread, for instance, she would put the light out and close the door. Yes, the Jehovah's Witnesses carried out their duties to the letter. They were prepared to take risks for Jehovah, but not for a fellow prisoner.

And yet one morning, before the usual distribution of bread— I had just completed a supplementary punishment of three food-less days for talking with the woman in the next cell, and I was lying half unconscious on the floor—the shutter in my door opened and a voice whispered breathlessly, "Grete, come quick, I've brought you something from Milena." I crawled on all fours to the door and pulled myself up. The woman pulled a small, squashed parcel out of her dress. "Take it quick. Milena sends you all her love. But hide it for the love of God." The shutter closed. I sank to the floor, the tears streaming down my cheeks. Milena hadn't forgotten me. She had sent me a handful of sugar, some bread, and two buns from a package she had received from home.

Dreams played an important part in concentration camp life. Strange to say, cheerful dreams were much more frequent among prisoners than among free persons. My own dreams, I might add, were often in color. But in the darkness of my cell I had dreams of a kind that were new to me, daydreams in which I escaped, not out into the camp but into true freedom. I was running with pounding heart through the narrow twilight streets of Berlin; I was in a hurry, because the train would soon be leaving for Prague, where Milena was expecting me. I went into a dismal shop, where in addition to great heaps of books there were reproductions of our favorite paintings. Brueghel in soft colors, impressionistic landscapes bathed in tremulous light. I leafed and rummaged and picked out one thing after another. Delighted with so many riches, I finally bought everything I could lay hands on. In the next shop I bought a fur-lined dressing gown. The fur was cinnamon color, made up of small pieces, some lighter, some darker, like the miraculous fur in the fairy tale.* I felt its warmth and softness and knew that it had curative power, that it would make Milena well again. I ran to the station with my treasure. The train was waiting, but I rushed to the newsstand and bought an armful of beautifully colored magazines. There were station sounds all around me; I breathed in the travel smells I loved so much. And then it all vanished. The light went on, the cell door was opened.

---

*"Thousandfurs" in *Grimms' Fairy Tales*.

Early one morning about two weeks later, the shutter in the iron door was opened again and the same Witness handed me a small parcel. Her face was convulsed with fear. I could see she was frantic. "Grete," she whispered, "I beg you, let me tell Milena that you don't want any more packages, it's too dangerous. Please, can I tell her that?" In the face of such terror, I could only consent. "Yes," I said, "I forbid Milena to send me anything more. I don't need anything." It was enough for me to know she was alive.

Later, at the end of my fifteen weeks in darkness, Milena told me how she had put pressure on the two Witnesses. Several times she had approached them on the camp street and begged them to bring me some bread. They had refused and left her flat. Then one evening she went to their barracks. She found out where their bunks were. On the third tier. She had trouble getting there with her bad leg but this time they could not escape. Again she implored them. You had to be really hard-hearted to resist Milena, but they were unmoved. Milena reminded them of all I had done for the Witnesses over the last two years. That too had no effect. Then she resorted to the language of Jehovah, the God of vengeance; she gave them a sermon on Christian charity and described the torments they could expect in the next world if they persisted in hardening their hearts. Whimpering, they promised to bring me the food she gave them.

One day I was taken from my dark cell to the prison office, and there stood a smiling Milena with Ramdor. My knees began to shake. I could think of only one explanation; now the beast had arrested Milena too. She guessed what I was thinking: "No," she said, "I haven't been arrested. I've only come to see how you were getting along. Everything is all right." Then I was brought back to my cell. For weeks I looked for an explanation. Could Ramdor have forced her to spy for him? Had she given him some information under questioning and been allowed to see me as her reward? No, that was impossible.

Even under normal conditions nothing is more dangerous to a concentration camp inmate than self-pity, than constant worry about his own personal fate. This is especially true in a dark cell. Terror gives way to apathy. I knew that if I was to survive I had to pull myself together and keep busy. I systematically divided the day into periods, each devoted to a different activity: walking, crawling, gymnastics, telling myself stories, reciting some of the countless poems I had had to learn in school, singing songs. In telling stories I took great pains not to leave anything out, and if I forgot a stanza of a poem I was reciting, I tried to make up one of my own and was very happy when I succeeded. But my storytelling was to take a dangerous turn.

I started retelling Maxim Gorki's story "A Man Is Born." The author tells us how as a boy he used to walk along the shore of the Black Sea near Sukhum, over roads and paths which I myself was to see forty years later, but under entirely different circumstances. One day, as he sat leaning against a tree at some distance from the path, waiting for the sun to rise over the sea, he saw dark forms against the light and heard the voices of people passing. It was a group of peasants, one of them a young woman, who along with many others had fled from the famine in the Orel district and found work near Sukhum.

The sun rises over the horizon and the boy follows the group. The path twines with the shoreline, and he soon loses sight of them. But then he sees something yellow in the bushes to one side. Coming closer, he hears moans and screams of pain. He runs to the woman's aid. He bends over her, sees her enormous quivering belly, sees her convulsed face, and realizes that she is in the throes of childbirth. He wants to help her, but she repulses him, crying out, "Go away! Have you no shame?" In her need, however, she accepts his assistance, and he helps a

191

new citizen of Orel into the world. He bathes the infant in the
sea and puts the wriggling little fellow into the mother's arms.
Then he makes a fire and makes tea for her. At the end of the
story the boy and the peasant woman follow the other peasants;
in one arm he carries the baby, with the other he supports her.

In retelling this story, a strange transformation occurred in
me. I couldn't drop it. A daydream took over, and the story
went on. I slipped into the skins of the protagonists. I myself
became the boy and the peasant woman, walking along the Black
Sea shore that I knew so well. From that point on I was two
people, two fugitives from reality. We found a hut on the edge
of a dense forest. A friendly place, though not much larger than
my cell; it, too, had no window, but it had a door that could
be opened. Now that there were two of me, I took twofold
pleasure in our refuge. My days now had a bright morning. I
went to the open door, looked out over the glittering sea, and
breathed the salt air. A happy ending in every respect. The
owner of the hut, a hunter, became our protector. There was
plenty of food, we were glad to be alive, we lay in the sun and
swam in the limpid water of the Black Sea. There was nothing
vague about the paradise I dreamed up; I relished every detail,
every hour, every minute of the day. I lost all sense of time and
reality, I no longer knew if it was morning or evening; I would
stay awake at night, because we were expecting a visit from the
hunter at midday and a meal had to be prepared for him. So
why bother about my bread ration when the table was groaning
under the choicest dishes?

The boy and the peasant woman loved each other, an idyll
of tender happiness. If only my neighbor wouldn't call me back
to reality by knocking on the wall between us. What were these
people to me? I shut my eyes and the boy took me in his arms
again.

One Sunday the cell door opened and I was released from the
Bunker. I hated the daylight and the ghastly reality. I wanted

to shut my eyes again and go back to my fantasies. I would have been lost without Milena's help. She understood the danger I was in, because mentally deranged inmates were put to death. She got me into the annex of the infirmary with a Czech *Blockälteste*. Whenever she could get away from her work, she came to see me. Over and over again I would tell her about the life of my heroes by the seashore, and she would listen with infinite patience. In this way she enabled me to return slowly to the reality of concentration camp life.

It was only then that I learned how she had come to visit me in the prison and what a risk she had run for my sake. For three weeks she had waited patiently for my return. She was afraid they might leave me to die there, and her fear grew from day to day. And then she made a heroic decision. She requested an appointment with Ramdor. Surprisingly enough, he agreed to see her. Possibly he expected her to denounce someone. He received her in his office, and she came right to the point. "I would like to speak to you about my friend Grete Buber. She is in the *Bunker*." It is unlikely that any other prisoner could have finished that sentence without getting at least a slap in the face. But Ramdor must have been affected by Milena's magic. He gave her a look of consternation but let her go on. "If you promise me," she said, "that Grete Buber will leave the *Bunker* alive, and that is in your power, I can do you a great service." Ramdor muttered something on the order of: "What the confounded . . . !" And Milena went on. "Horrible things are happening in this camp. If nothing is done to stop them, you can say good-bye to your career." That was too much. Ramdor pushed his chair back from the desk and went red in the face. "Who do you think you're talking to!" he blustered. "I beg your pardon," said Milena, "you don't seem to understand. I've only come here to help you. My asking a favor of you is something else again. If you're not interested in what I have to tell you, I beg your pardon. Just send me back to the infirmary."

It's a wonder that Milena wasn't taken directly to the *Bunker*. But she brazened it out, and in the end Ramdor gave her an opening. "What are these horrible things that are happening?" he asked. Milena kept him in suspense for as long as possible. "Serious criminal offenses," she said. "Both prisoners and members of the SS are involved. But before I give you the details, I want to know whether you are prepared to meet my conditions?" "What is this impertinence? Do you think you can blackmail me?" "Of course not, Herr Kriminalassistent. How could I, a mere prisoner, think anything of the kind? But I thought that you, as a German, would know the meaning of friendship. Tell me, would you abandon a friend in such a situation?"

Ramdor turned to face her. She had succeeded in touching some chord in this scoundrel and was quick to follow through. "Can you tell me if Grete Buber is still alive?" "Of course she is." "Can I see her? This very day?" "Take it easy. Don't go too far."

Milena started telling him what kind of person I was. Ramdor made his next mistake. He listened, and that enabled her to go on with her seduction program. When at last he had given her his word of honor to keep his promise, she told him what crimes were being committed day and night in the infirmary. Of course this was nothing new to Ramdor and of course he did not find it revolting. He himself was a murderer. But this was a threat to his career. It would have been his duty to expose Dr. Rosenthal, because in the eyes of the Gestapo it was a crime for a member of the SS to sell the gold teeth of the dead for his own private profit. So Ramdor stepped in and before long the medical officer and his mistress were arrested.

But what would have happened to Milena if Ramdor had chosen to cover Dr. Rosenthal? She would have been shot that same day. Of that she was well aware, but it did not deter her. Buoyed by the momentum of her onslaught, she forgot the burden of her sick body. But when she got back to the infirmary, her weakness gained the upper hand, and she was paralyzed with fear that Quernheim would come and kill her with one of her lethal injections.

Some months later Ramdor tried to blackmail Milena. He came to the infirmary, sent for her, and asked her to spy on one of the prisoners. "Herr Ramdor," she said, "you've come to the wrong address. I am not a stool pigeon." Ramdor gulped. And then he made the astonishing remark: "I can't deny it. You really are a decent person." And Milena shot back: "Yes, I am. And I didn't need you to tell me."

After my release from the *Bunker*, I found out what had become of Senior Overseer Langefeld. On the day after my arrest, she was allowed to go to her office. On the way, she had a conversation with Milena, who rushed up to her and implored her to save me from death. Though Langefeld promised Milena to do everything in her power, she knew that her own hour had struck. That same day she was put under house arrest and separated from her child. She spent the next day in strict isolation in her apartment. Her only thought was to let someone know what was happening to her. Late that afternoon she heard a column of prisoners singing as they marched past on their way back from work. She leaped to the window, opened it, and shouted at the top of her lungs, "Help!" The SS man who was guarding her dragged her away from the window.

The next day the order for her arrest arrived from Berlin. She was taken to Breslau, her last place of residence, and tried by an SS tribunal. The charge against her was that she had been "a tool of the Polish political prisoners and had shown sympathy for Polish nationalists." The hearings went on for fifty days, at the end of which she was acquitted for lack of proof and dismissed from Ravensbrück.

21

HER LAST BIRTHDAY

To want death but not the pain of dying is a bad sign. Except for that, death can be faced.

—KAFKA, *BRIEFE AN MILENA*

One of the most dreaded institutions in Ravensbrück was the "labor mobilization." Every day labor gangs were formed to work in munitions or other war-connected factories or in the construction of airfields. Every prisoner hoped to stay in the main camp and to avoid being shipped to the annexes, in most of which the food was much worse.

After my recovery, for fear of being shipped out, I looked around for a "good" outside job in the main camp. Some Polish prisoners who knew me offered me a job in the logging gang, and I accepted gladly. The prisoner in charge, Mother Liberak, as the Poles called her, was an angel, and from time to time each member of the crew was given a day off. A week later my turn came. It was a sunny day in the late fall. I couldn't bear to stay shut up in the barracks and Milena had errands in various parts of the camp, so I joined her. This was risky, but as Milena was wearing the yellow armband of an infirmary worker, the camp police didn't bother us.

We walked about, deep in conversation. On one side, we could see the last yellow leaves at the top of a willow tree on the far side of the wall, on the other, there were dark pine trees. We talked about the forests and cities we planned to see together someday and about the loved ones who were waiting for us. On the outside, life was going on; perhaps our children, who would soon be young girls, had forgotten us. Fear of the censorship had reduced the few letters we received from outside into impersonal stereotypes. "I really know nothing about Honza," said Milena sadly. "If only she would tell me the color of her dress or whether she's started to wear silk stockings, or what she does on some particular day. If she'd only stop telling me that she goes to school and likes to play the piano." Milena worried about the child, she reproached herself for having involved Honza in her own private and political life so young. And now this independent, precocious child was having to contend with her grandfather, who must be treating her as capriciously and tyrannically as he had treated her mother. In his letters he referred to his granddaughter as *pohanka*, the little pagan, and Milena gathered from certain cautious hints that Honza had run away from him and had been getting into trouble with various sets of foster parents. What Milena did not know was how very much the child's grandfather admired her courage and strength of character, because not even the Gestapo had succeeded in making her talk.

Milena showed me her father's latest letter, which expressed only worry and real affection. In a mellow mood that day, she said, "My father's love for his own flesh and blood had a strange way of expressing itself, but it can't be helped. He's a tyrant and that's that." Then she spoke of his good qualities, how splendidly he had behaved when the Germans marched into Prague. And she also had pleasant childhood memories connected with him. He was an enthusiastic skier; he had taught her to ski at a time when such activities were unusual for women and he had taken her on marvelous skiing trips. With a group

197

of his students and often with his old friend Matuš, he had led her through the wintry beauty of the Bohemian forest. "To look at me now," she said, "you wouldn't believe that I was once one of the best woman skiers in the country. I even tried to keep it up with my stiff knee."

As we were turning back at the end of the camp street, we were horrified to catch sight of Dittman, head of the labor mobilization service. Before he had even reached us he started bellowing, "What are you doing here during working hours?" He remembered me from Langefeld's office and knew about all my "crimes." "Why haven't you reported for labor mobilization?" he shouted at me. His face, which owed its special character to a boil on one cheek, went purple with rage. "I'm sick," I said. "I've been assigned to inside duty." That was the only lie that occurred to me. Luckily, he left Milena alone because of her yellow armband. "You haven't been in the *Bunker* for quite a while, have you? Report to the labor mobilization office this minute or the fur will fly." His top boots creaked as he turned to go.

When I got there, Dittman called me into his private office and belabored me with dire threats. In the end he ordered me to report to the tailor shop for punitive work on the assembly line. "Report to Oberscharführer Graf. I'll phone him to expect you. Get going!"

On August 10, 1943, Milena's Czech friends showed their affection for her. Suspecting that this would be her last birthday, they decided to give her a real party. In the orderly room of a barracks with a Czech *Blockälteste*, the table was covered with presents. All those who loved Milena were present: Anička Kvapilová, Tomy Kleinerová, Nina the dancer, Milena Fischerová, the writer, Hana Feierabendová, Mana Opočenská, Manja Svediková, Bertel Schindlerová, and others whose names I have forgotten. Someone went to get the birthday child and she was led to the table. The gifts consisted of handkerchiefs embroidered with a prisoner's number, tiny cloth hearts marked with the name "Milena," figurines carved from toothbrush handles, flowers that had been smuggled into camp.

Milena, who was very ill by then and too weak to keep up all her friendships, was moved to tears: "What a surprise!" she said. "And I thought you'd all forgotten me and weren't friends with me anymore. Forgive me for not coming to see you more often. But from now on I'll be better." Surrounded by her Czech friends, Milena was all joy and gratitude. I, the "little Prussian," stood a little to one side, watching the others laugh, enjoying the unusual atmosphere. I felt transported to Prague, to Milena's natural surroundings. What Milena wanted most in the world was to have friends. She once wrote: "If you have two or three people, but what am I saying, if you have just one person with whom you can be weak, miserable, and contrite, and who won't hurt you for it, then you are rich. You can expect indulgence only of one who loves you, never from others and, above all, never from yourself."

22

MILENA'S END

The winter of 1944 was hard in Ravensbrück. We knew what was happening at the fronts, we knew that Hitler's star was on the wane, but many of the inmates were at the end of their strength, they needed to be rescued in days or weeks. But we had to stick it out, to look on helplessly while each day exacted new victims.

In the early years of the camp, the dead were taken away in a rustic horse-drawn hearse driven by Herr Wendland of the Wendland Trucking Company. As more and more inmates died, Herr Wendland's business thrived and he bought a motorized hearse. But then the first crematorium was built, and the SS went into the undertaking business. What was the need of coffins? Simple crates would do. Why waste a whole crate on a single body? The bodies were so thin, there was plenty of room for two. In the early days the infirmary workers would carry the dead through the camp gate—now, with more than fifty deaths a day, crate after crate was loaded onto a flat-topped truck and driven to the crematorium.

That winter Milena's condition grew worse from day to day. Her resistance was broken. She dragged herself to work for fear of being given a lethal injection or being shipped to a death camp. But she kept collapsing. She felt she was losing her moral fiber and despised herself for being more and more willing to compromise. She often spoke of death. "I'll never get out of this camp alive, I'll never see Prague again. If at least Herr Wendland would be taking me away. He looks so good-natured in his peasant jacket."

After the arrest of Dr. Rosenthal, a new SS medical officer took over. This was Dr. Percy Treite, whose mother was an Englishwoman. At the same time, some doctors from among the prisoners were allowed to work in the infirmary, which seemed to lose its terrors. Dr. Treite was distinguished from his predecessors by his good manners. He inspired confidence, especially after he had set up a separate barracks for mothers and their infants. It looked as if the babies born in Ravensbrück would now be allowed to live. But then they would have to be fed. Dr. Treite applied to the camp commander for a milk ration, as their undernourished mothers were unable to nurse them. He meant well, but the camp commander turned down his application, and all the newborn babies starved to death. It is hard to say whether Dr. Treite, who held a low rank in the SS, could have put pressure on the camp commander.

Milena made Dr. Treite's acquaintance in the infirmary, and he treated her with great consideration. He told her that while studying in Prague he had attended Professor Jan Jesensky's lectures, and that gave her confidence in him. She told him about her illness. He examined her and found that one of her kidneys was ulcerated. The only hope, he said, was to have it removed. Milena decided to risk it. She was admitted to the infirmary in January 1944. Treite gave her a blood transfusion. When I went to see her at midday, she was overjoyed and showed me her hands. "They're all pink," she said. "Like a healthy person's."

During the operation she had awoken from the anesthetic and asked Treite to let her see her kidney. He did, and she was put to sleep again.

During the noon break I ran to the infirmary, where she lay

201

silent and deathly pale. Still under the influence of the anesthetic, she lifted up her voice and solemnly said the Lord's Prayer in Czech.

She survived the operation and her condition even improved. She thought she was going to get better and recaptured her will to live. For the six dying women in her ward she once again became Mother Milena, whose mere presence sufficed to give them strength. A package came from her father. She distributed the contents, which made for a festive atmosphere in the dismal room. Across from her lay a French girl, hardly more than a child, who was dying. She couldn't bear the camp food. Her eyes sparkled at the sight of Milena's delicacies, she ate a little, and began to sing the "Marseillaise": "Allons, Enfants de la Patrie"; the others joined in.

For four months my day had no other content than the quarter of an hour spent at Milena's bedside. Before the morning roll call, while it was still dark, I ran to the infirmary with some breakfast for her. At noon I hurried to a distant barracks with a Czech *Blockälteste* to warm some food for her. Then I would sit with her, hiding my anguish and doing my best to radiate optimism. Of course I was forbidden to set foot in the infirmary, but I felt that nothing could happen, that some mysterious power was protecting me.

One day Milena got up and went down the corridor to her office; she wanted to sit at her desk once again; from there she could look out at the world of freedom through the bars of the camp gate.

But her remission was brief. She was soon too weak to get out of bed. From where she lay she could see a patch of sky, sometimes traversed by friendly, more often by menacing, cloud formations. Vera Papoušková, another Czech friend, gave her a deck of cards that she herself had made, little works of art. We played cards to dispel our dark thoughts. Snatches of song broke the silence of the sickroom; a passing column of prisoners were singing: "The roses are blooming in my country, that's where I long to be. . . ." Milena buried her face in her hands and wept.

In April, Milena's other kidney became ulcerated and all hope was gone. In my despair I prayed to the sun and the stars, but all in vain. The more her condition deteriorated, the more convinced Milena became that she would recover. Not until the last few days did she recognize the truth: "Look at the color of my feet," she said. "Those are the feet of a dying woman. And the hands!" She held out her hands. "The lines are disappearing. That's what happens just before the end."

At short intervals her father sent her three postcards, romantic views of Prague by Morstadt in the Biedermeier style. Milena looked at the old engravings and on the brink of death guided me through Prague. Pointing at one of the postcards, she would say: "This bridge, I often crossed it with my friend Fredy Mayer. He had an eye for beauty . . . That's Saint John of Nepomuk on the parapet . . . and those narrow streets back there, they lead to the big marketplace. . . ." We looked at the magnificent façade of a church with two tall spires; the door was hidden by a colonnade. Milena's finger pointed at an old fountain; four angels with drawn swords were standing on its rim. "Come this way," she said. "That little street still has its dear old bumpy cobblestones." We passed through a gateway into the courtyard of a palace, surrounded by tiers of arcades. . . . Later we came to a church tower. The three of us started up the spiral stairway. . . . "Not so fast. You know I have trouble climbing stairs with my stiff leg. So does Fredy for that matter." I looked up and saw her faraway look. She had burst the bonds of captivity. She was at home with Fredy and me, looking down through the embrasure at the top of a tower at her beloved city with its hundreds of steeples, its maze of gabled roofs, its little streets and courtyards and sleeping places. Then she shook herself, picked up her father's latest letter, speaking of the beautiful spring day and his morning walks in the Kinsky Gardens, and said sadly, "Why doesn't *Tata* say more?"

One more card came from her father. In it, for Milena's sake, he told a lie. He told her that Honza had passed her examination at the Conservatory. But Milena—who may have seen through his falsehood—turned away and read no more.

On May 15, 1944, packages were distributed, and I was sent for. There was a big box for Milena from Joachim von Zedtwitz. I ran to Milena with it. She was not fully conscious, but when she heard the name of Zedtwitz she sat up. Her eyes were failing and she made me read the name again and again. Then she sank back with a happy sigh and cried out, "Thank God he's alive. It's a miracle. I thought he had been shot."

Joachim von Zedtwitz, who had been arrested soon after Milena, was released at the end of 1943 when a well-placed uncle had vouched for him. Though still under police surveillance, he got in touch with Milena's father, found out which camp she was in, and prevailed on a Berlin lawyer to apply for a pardon for her. The lawyer wrote to Prague for the necessary documents, and all was in readiness when a bomb fell on the lawyer's house and killed him.

Later, that same afternoon while I was at work, someone came and told me that Milena was dying. I ran out of my work station without considering the possible consequences of such an act. What could happen to me now? Milena was in a state of euphoria. She was radiant, her dark-blue eyes were shining, and when I went up to her, she held out her arms in that beautiful gesture of hers. She was no longer able to speak. Her Czech friends were surrounding her; some by her bed, others stood outside, at the window. Milena looked blissfully at them all and took her leave of life. In the evening she lost consciousness. She died two days later, on May 17. Only then did I go back to my barracks. Life had lost all meaning for me.

When the disposal squad loaded Milena's coffin onto the truck, I asked leave to ride to the crematorium with them. It was a spring day, a warm rain was falling. The sentry at the camp gate may have thought it was rain running down my cheeks. A water bird was piping sadly in the rushes on the bank of Lake Fürstenberg. We unloaded the crates and carried them to the crematorium. Two male criminals with faces like hangmen removed the lids. As we were carrying Milena's body, my strength failed me. One of them said contemptuously, "Get a good hold on her. She can't feel anything."

On Dr. Treite's order, Milena's body was left in the vestibule of the crematorium. He had sent Dr. Jesensky a telegram, notifying him of his daughter's death and informing him that he could have her remains sent to Prague.

On June 10, 1944, news of the successful Normandy landing reached the camp. I was unable to share in the general rejoicing. I grieved all day and cried all night. Why go on living when Milena was dead?

Not long after Milena's death, when conditions in the camp were growing more and more chaotic and the prisoners were torn between hope and fear, Anička, whom I had been seeing every day, asked me to go in the evening to a certain place along the wall, not far from the men's camp. A large number of Czech women had gathered there. They sang the Czech national anthem, hoping the men on the other side of the wall might hear them and respond. Years before, at a time of great danger, Milena had written: "This anthem isn't against anyone. 'Kde domov muj' wishes no one any harm, all it wants is that we may continue to exist. It is not a battle hymn, it merely celebrates the countryside of Bohemia with its hills and dales, its fields and meadows, its birches, willows, and shady lindens, its fragrant hedgerows and little brooks. It celebrates the country that is our home . . . How beautiful it was to stand up for our country and to love it."*

I recovered my freedom and carried out Milena's last will by writing *our* book about concentration camps. Shortly before her death she had said to me one day: "I know that you at least will not forget me. Through you I shall live on. You will tell people who I was, you are my indulgent judge. . . ." Those words gave me the courage to write her story.

*Milena Jesenská, "On the Art of Standing Still."

BIOGRAPHICAL NOTES*

BLEI, Franz: Director of various magazines (such as the *Hyperion* of Munich), translator, publicist, author of comedies, discoverer of Musil and Robert Walser.

BŘEZÍNA, Otakar (1868–1929): Czech poet; one of the greatest European symbolists.

BROCH, Hermann (1886–1951): Austrian novelist steeped in the German literary tradition; depicted the decay of bourgeois values in the Germany of William II. Emigrated to the United States after the *Anschluss*.

ČAPEK, Karel (1890–1938): One of Czechoslovakia's greatest writers in the twentieth century. Considered a symbol of his friend Masaryk's liberal republic. Published many novels and plays dealing with the perils threatening humanity and democracy; criticized dehumanization and mechanization in industrial society (he coined the word "robot") and also the fascist menace. His wife, the actress and writer Olga Scheinpflugová, was the author of numerous plays and novels inspired by the lives of women.

EHRENSTEIN, Albert (1886–1950): Poet, close to German expressionism; Karl Kraus's collaborator. A great traveler, his travel writings reflect a strong anticolonialism. In 1932, he settled in Switzerland,

*The notes were prepared by Alain Brossat with the help of Vladimir Peška.

207

and in 1941 he emigrated to the United States, where he died in utter poverty.

EISNER, Pavel (1889–1958): Translated Kafka, Rilke, Mann, and others into Czech and such Czech writers as Březína and Halas into German.Wrote critical essays about the poet Mácha, Mozart, the Czech language, and so on.

FISCHER, Otakar (1883–1938): Sensitive and highly cultured, this professor of German literature was also a celebrated translator (of Kleist, Heine, Nietszche, Goethe, Shakespeare, Kipling, Calderón, Corneille, Villon, etc.), a playwright as well as the artistic director of the Czech National Theater, a literary critic, and a poet. Died of a heart attack when he learned of Hitler's occupation of Austria.

FUCHS, Rudolf (born in 1890): A Prague poet who published *The Caravan* at Kurt Wolff in 1918. A friend of Kafka.

FUČIK, Julius (1903–1943): Newspaperman and literary critic, as well as militant Communist. Arrested by the Nazis and executed for underground activities.

GERSTL, Alice: Followed Otto Rühle in exile to Mexico. Killed herself the day he died, in 1943. Wrote a book of memoirs about Leon Trotsky, *Kein Gedicht für Trotzki* (Verlag Neue Kritik, 1979).

GROSS, Otto (1877–1919): Austrian psychoanalyst who studied with Freud. Fervent advocate of free love.

HAAS, Willy: Czech writer. Friend of Milena. Edited and wrote introduction to Franz Kafka's *Letters to Milena*.

HAŠEK, Jaroslav (1863–1923): Anarchist, then Communist, fought in Russia during the revolution (about which he wrote *Adventures in the Red Army*). Also a newspaperman, the author of many humorous and satirical stories, creator of the archetypal figure of Svejk (Schweik).

HOFFMEISTER, Adolf (1902–1973): Prose writer, dramatist, poet, cartoonist, illustrator, caricaturist, he was a member of Devétsil, the cultural association of the left, and had ties to surrealism. During the war, directed the Czechoslovak radio in exile in the United States. After the Prague coup, he was successively ambassador to France (1948–52), professor, delegate to UNESCO. He was sympathetic to the Prague Spring, taught at the University of Vincennes near Paris, and, forbidden to publish, died in his native land.

HORA, Josef (1891–1945): Newspaperman, Communist, then Liberal; translator of poetry from Russian, German, Serbo-Croatian; for a time novelist; he was above all one of the great Czech poets of this century.

JESENSKÁ, Ružena (1863–1940): Milena perfectly characterizes the writings of her aunt, which included more than fifty collections of poetry, volumes of short stories, novels, plays, and children's books.

KALANDRA, Závis (1902–1950): Newspaperman, former leader of the Czech Communist Student League, he was expelled from the Czech Communist party for having criticized the Moscow trials. During the 1930s founded a newspaper with Trotskyist leanings. A historian of the Czech nation, he was arrested by the Nazis late in 1939 and imprisoned at Ravensbrück. He pursued the study of history after the war, but during the first Stalinist purges in postwar Czechoslovakia was tried and executed for "high treason and espionage."

KISCH, Egon Erwin (1885–1948): Czech newspaperman who rallied to communism after a trip to the USSR in 1928. Lived in exile in France after the advent of fascism, participated in the Spanish Civil War, took refuge in Mexico, died in London.

KODIČEK, Josef (1892–1954): Theater critic, literary theorist, scriptwriter, and film director. After Munich, expatriated himself in London, where he directed the BBC's Czech broadcasts. Took part in Radio Free Europe broadcasts from Munich after 1948.

KORNFELD, Paul (1889–1942): Prague-born dramatist, author of major works of expressionism in the theater. Died in a concentration camp in Poland.

KRAUS, Karl (1874–1936): Austrian writer, founder in 1899 of the magazine *Die Fackel (The Flame)*, in which he assumed the role of pitiless judge of social, political, and cultural life in Austria. He produced many volumes of verse, aphorisms, translations, dramas. A pacifist, he wrote a play against war (*The Last Days of Mankind*, 1914) and a violent indictment of Nazism (*The Third Night of Walpurgis*, not published until 1952).

KREJČÁR, Jaromír (1895–1950): Studied under one of the fathers of modern Czech architecture, Jan Kotera, espoused ideas of the Constructivist avant-garde (Le Corbusier), realized few of the many projects he conceived. His bohemian marriage to Milena was dissolved while he was in Russia, from which he returned disillusioned. Died in London.

KŘIČKA, Petr (1884–1949): Traditional poet who wrote movingly of such collective and individual Czech experiences as those of the soldiers in the Great War.

LOOS, Adolf (1870–1933): Architect born in Moravia, established in business in Vienna, he had ties to Bauhaus and became one of the pioneers of modern architecture.

MASARYK, Tomáš Guarrigue (1850–1937): Czech politician, philosopher, and sociologist. Fought on the side of the Allies in World War I. Was elected president of the republic in 1918, reelected in 1927 and 1934. Resigned in 1935 for health reasons.

MAY, Ernst (1886–1970): German architect who spent 1930 to 1933 working in the USSR as an urban planner. Emigrated to Nairobi, Kenya, returned to Germany after World War II.

MEYER, Hannes (1889–1954): Swiss architect, succeeded Gropius as the head of Bauhaus, spent 1930 to 1936 working in the USSR as an urban planner, then returned to Switzerland.

MOLNÁR, Franz (1878–1952): Novelist and playwright born in Budapest, successful as an author of ironic comedies in Europe between the two wars. After the Nazis came to power, emigrated to the United States. *Liliom* is his most famous play.

NEMCOVÁ, Božena (1820–1862): Among the most popular of Czech women of letters. An early proponent of national cultural emancipation, she recorded the daily lives of the people, collected and updated Czech and Slovak fairy tales, wrote numerous narratives concerning the difficult destinies of young women. *Grandmother* (1855) was her chef d'oeuvre.

NEUMANN, Heinz (1902–1937): A director of the German Communist party, one of the organizers of the abortive insurrection of 1923. Represented the party in Moscow in 1925, was sent in 1927 on a mission to China, where he was one of the organizers of the Canton commune. Editor in chief of the party paper, *Die Rote Fahne*, in 1928. After he opposed Stalin's policies in 1932, was divested of his responsibilities and sent to Spain. Acknowledged his divisiveness in an auto-critique in 1934. Was arrested in Switzerland, deported to the USSR, arrested there in April 1937, and executed without trial.

NEUMANN, Stanislav Kostka (1875–1947): Writer of bourgeois origins whose creative itinerary included "decadent" symbolism; anarchic individualism; the exaltation of life, nature, and modern civilization; and communism, which he abandoned for a time in 1929 before taking up a certain popular traditionalism.

NEZVAL, Viteslav (1900–1958): Principal poet of the "Poetist" avant-garde, then surrealist. Abandoned surrealism in 1938 on orders from the party and was poet laureate of the Communist regime after 1948.

OUD, Jacobus Johannes Piter (1890–1963): Dutch architect, founder of the de Stijl movement.

PEROUTKA, Ferdinand (1893–1978): Great liberal and democratic newspaperman in the tradition of Karel Havlícek, the inflexible adversary of the Hapsburgs; also literary critic and historian. After six years' imprisonment in Buchenwald, he resumed his journalistic activities, but chose exile in the United States after the Prague coup.

PFEMFERT, Franz: Publisher of the weekly, *Die Aktion*, founded in 1911, he encouraged the new, nonconformist, revolutionary tendencies of the young artists associated most notably with expressionism. Was radically opposed to patriotic and chauvinistic trends among intellectuals before and during World War I.

PICK, Otto (1887–1940): Editor on the daily, *Prager Presse*, and translator of numerous Czech dramatists, notably Karel Čapek.

PREISLER, Jan (1872–1918): Important proponent of a strongly symbolist, expressive, and poetic art nouveau.

RÜHLE, Otto (1874–1943): Professor, psychologist, pedagogue. Militant in various left-wing parties including the SPD and KPD from 1900 to 1933, when he emigrated. Moved to Mexico in 1936. There established close relations with Leon Trotsky.

SCHLAMM, Willi: First publisher of the German leftist magazine, *Weltbühne*, in emigration. Tried to maintain a leftist socialist line without rallying to the KPD. Was dismissed in 1934 for having published a text by Trotsky.

ŠRÁMEK, Fraňá (1877–1952): Poet, novelist, dramatist who exalted young, fragile, sensitive souls free of prejudice and convention. In his anarchist youth, Šrámek was aligned with S. K. Neumann; after the war, more resigned and melancholic, he moved closer to Karel Čapek.

ŠTURSA, Jan (1886–1925): Student, then assistant, of the great classicist of Czech sculpture, Myslbek, he was able to evolve and open new vistas thanks to lessons gleaned from Michelangelo, Rodin, Maillol, and Bourdelle. Notable works include busts of Smetana and Masaryk.

SVOBODOVA, Ružena (1868–1920): Important Czech novelist and short story writer who responded to dry realism and naturalism with a romantically tinged impressionism.

TEIGE, Karel (1900–1951): Art critic and theoretician, cofounder of the Devétsil group, then editor of numerous art and cultural magazines. Expert in matters of architecture and urban planning, with ties to Bauhaus. Member of the Czech Communist party who made many trips to the USSR after 1925.

URZIDIL, Johannes (1896–1970): Native of Prague. Press attaché at the German embassy. Knew Kafka, Brod, and so on. Left Germany with his wife, a Jew, in 1939 and moved to the United States. His works included essays, narratives, novels.

VANČURA, Vladislav (1891–1942): A director of Devétsil, he left the Communist party in 1929 but rejoined later. An important innovator in prose and the theater. After the assassination of Heydrich he was arrested as a member of the resistance; was executed shortly after the extermination of the village of Lidice.

WELTSCH, Felix: Philosopher from Prague, friend of Kafka and Brod. Editor in chief of Prague's Zionist weekly, *Selbstwehr* (*Self-Defense*).

WERFEL, Franz (1890–1945): Expressionist novelist; a native of Prague. In 1912 published *Die Weltfreund* (*The Friend of the World*) and went on to write many novels, novellas, and short stories. Worked for the publisher Kurt Wolff, where he brought together poets of the expressionist generation. From 1915 to 1917 a soldier in the Austrian army. Met and wed Alma Mahler, widow of Gustave Mahler, in Vienna. Emigrated to France after Hitler's invasion of Austria, and from there to the United States, where he died.

Niemandsland (*No-Man's-Land*): film by Victor Trivas, based on an idea by Leonard Frank, 1931.